WRITING GREAT TOM
T. S. Eliot & the Keepers of the Flame

WRITING GREAT TOM
T. S. Eliot & the Keepers of the Flame

By

T. S. Matthews

Foreword by Sara Fitzgerald

Karen Christensen, Editor

BERKSHIRE PUBLISHING GROUP
Great Barringon, Massachusetts

© Berkshire Publishing Group LLC 2024
All rights reserved

No part of this book may be reproduced or utilized in any form or by any means, electronic or mechanical, including photocopying, recording, or by any information storage and retrieval system, without permission in writing from the publisher.

Educators: Contact us if you want to post material from this book online for your students. Teachers at institution that own a print copy may use up to 10 copies per course or program at no charge, but the right to copy additional pages for distribution in print or via any online platform is granted only with the agreement of the publisher and/or payment of appropriate fees to Copyright Clearance Center, www.copyright.com. Inquiries to cservice@berkshirepublishing.com will be promptly answered.

Translation rights & other permissions: Write to cservice@berkshirepublishing.com with details of the rights or permission sought.

Quantity orders: Discounts up to 40%, depending on quantity, are available from the publisher.

Berkshire Publishing Group LLC
122 Castle Street, Great Barrington, Massachusetts 01230 USA
www.berkshirepublishing.com

Library of Congress Cataloging-in-Publication Data

Names: Matthews, T. S. (Thomas Stanley), 1901–1991, author. | Fitzgerald, Sara, writer of foreword. | Christensen, Karen, writer of afterword.
Title: Writing Great Tom : T. S. Eliot & the keepers of the flame / by T. S. Matthews.
Description: Great Barrington, Massachusetts: Berkshire Publishing Group, [2024] | Includes bibliographical references and index.
Identifiers: LCCN 2022037513 | ISBN 9781614720591 (hardback) | ISBN 9781614720607 (paperback) | ISBN 9781614720614 (epub)
Subjects: LCSH: Matthews, T. S. (Thomas Stanley), 1901–1991. Great Tom. | Eliot, T. S. (Thomas Stearns), 1888–1965. | Poets, American—20th century—Biography—History and criticism. | Biography as a literary form.
Classification: LCC PS3509.L43 .Z7373 2024 | DDC 821/.912
[B]—dc23/eng/20221006
LC record available at https://lccn.loc.gov/2022037513

ISBN – 9781614720591 hardcover
ISBN – 9781614720607 paperback
ISBN – 9781614720614 ebook

Thank you to Sara Fitzgerald for alerting us to the existence of the Matthews collection at Princeton, to the Firestone Library staff for their kind assistance, both remote and in person, and to Christopher Matthews and Alexander Matthews for their help and permission to make this document available.

CONTENTS

Foreword .... *vii*
Editor's Note .... *xix*

Introduction: Living a Detective Story 3
Meetings with TSE 15
1970 25
1971 53
1972 177

Afterword by Karen Christensen *217*
About the Author *223*
Foreword Author *224*
Index *225*
About the Type *230*

FOREWORD

By Sara Fitzgerald

The year was 1970—and five years after his death, the poet T. S. Eliot was still an international literary phenomenon. As friends and colleagues considered whether to capture their memories and sell them, an enterprising editor at Harper & Row in New York approached a close friend of hers about writing a book.

"I have had a SIGN," Frances Lindley[1] wrote T. S. Matthews on January 9, the sort of thing, she observed, "that Eliot's magi needed so desperately." Would Matthews drop everything he was doing and write "the biography of Tom Eliot which no one else is equipped to do. . . the non-graduate school, non-Marxist, non-Freudian book which only an American poet out of the American Middle West into the Eastern cultural cooker over to England, etc., etc. could do."[2]

---

[1] Frances to "Dearest Tom," January 9, 1970, T. S. Matthews Papers, Series 3: Correspondence 1931–1990, Lindley, Frances, Box 27, Folder 7. By the time of her death, Lindley was a legendary editor, credited for nurturing such diverse best-sellers as Erich Segal's *Love Story* and Aleksandr Solzhenitsyn's *Gulag Archipelago*.

[2] Unless otherwise specified, quotations from Matthews come from this manuscript, *Writing Great Tom*, or the foreword and acknowledgements of *Great Tom*.

Matthews had interviewed Eliot and met him on various occasions, and admired the late Nobel laureate. They had more in common than just their names and initials. Matthews too came from a socially prominent family, had gone to an Ivy League college and then Oxford. After resigning his post as editor of *TIME* magazine over its coverage of the 1952 presidential campaign of his Princeton classmate, Adlai Stevenson, he moved to England and tried to start a British version of the magazine. After the project fell apart, he remained in England for the rest of his life.

Lindley stressed to Matthews that she was serious and added, "PLEASE, PLEASE, PLEASE. TAKE THREE YEARS, FOUR YEARS. PLEASE."

Matthews was intrigued by the offer. But from the outset, he was concerned about whether Valerie Eliot, the poet's widow, would cooperate. (Valerie Fletcher had been thirty years old when, after eight years as his secretary, she married the sixty-eight-year-old Eliot in 1957.) Winthrop Knowlton, executive vice president of Harper & Row, quickly stepped in and broached the question on Matthews's behalf.

Mrs. Eliot was quick to respond. On January 29, 1970, she sent a terse reply on Faber and Faber letterhead: "I cannot give you the slightest encouragement or help with your proposed biography of my husband, because he forbade one in a memorandum with his Will. In time, of course, such a book must be written, but in accordance with my husband's wishes I cannot assist such a project."[3]

But Matthews decided to proceed anyway. He signed a contract, promising to deliver a manuscript in three years. He received an advance against royalties of $2,750—or about $22,000 in today's dollars—and another $3,000 to cover his expenses.[4]

---

3   Valerie Eliot to Winthrop Knowlton, January 29, 1970, Lindley Correspondence.
4   T. S. Matthews to John Jay Iselin, May 31, 1970, Lindley Correspondence. In this letter, Matthews explained the arrangements he had made with his executors for handling these advances if his ill health prevented him from delivering the manuscript.

After Matthews sent out letters to publications such as the Harvard alumni magazine, seeking persons with memories of Eliot, he was approached by eleven other publishers who were interested in his book. His editor hoped that the Book of the Month Club might adopt it as a main selection.

Matthews began by submerging himself in Eliot's life, reading all or part of about eighty books on the poet and 216 items in Donald Gallup's bibliography of Eliot's work. By the end of the first year, he had collected twenty-three folders of notes and a correspondence file with several hundred letters. Like most of *TIME's* male journalists, he relied on women researchers to do most of his legwork. Some of his interviews turned into social engagements, accompanied by his wife. This enabled him, when he eventually began to write the book, to sprinkle his narrative with anecdotes from unnamed sources, but no footnotes—except for the citations of published materials that Harper & Row's lawyers demanded.

But at the age seventy, Matthews was also challenged by health problems and a reluctance to travel back to the States, where most of the details of Eliot's early life were hidden. More importantly, he was frustrated by Mrs. Eliot's continued opposition, her instructions to friends and family members not to cooperate with him, and the control she exercised over Eliot-related materials housed at major research libraries. He was constantly worried about getting "scooped" by other Eliot memoirists or by a biography authorized by Mrs. Eliot.

Midway through the project, he reflected, "I can say that I'm getting used to Eliot's poems, though I can't honestly say I understand them. And what are the prospects? Well, (1) to write Eliot's life, based on the scraps I can scavenge from the garbage pails in the area-ways, and to finish it no later than a year from now, to make sure that I'm not beaten to the draw by Valerie and Fabers' change of mind, and their appointing an official biographer: 2) to write it without being allowed to quote one line of Eliot's poetry or a phrase of his critical writing: or 3) to cut the losses. . . ." (That sentence drops off, tantalizingly, on a page-break of Matthews's somewhat disorganized journal.)

Early on, Matthews interviewed Frank Morley, Eliot's close friend and colleague and the Eliot confidante Matthews said he most wanted to meet. Afterwards, Morley demonstrated his skills as an editor by observing that Matthews really didn't know what kind of book he wanted to write: "Is it a detached study of this particular man as a kind of phenomenon and of the rise and decline and (who knows?) resurgence from time to time of Eliot cults? Is it a personal essay, how you got interested in Eliot (same initials, some similarity of situation as one American who lives in England writing of another) and why you set yourself to puzzle him out and what estimate you have come to as to the man and his work? . . . What sort of catalog description has Harper got in mind? What public have you in mind?"

Matthews quickly confessed that he wished he knew the answers to those questions. "A detached study? Hmm. Well, semi-detached—thanks to Mrs. Eliot. A personal essay? Ah, now you may be getting warmer. But I can't answer your questions without largely making up the answers as I go along, for I simply don't know."[5]

Matthews later wrote that the "one interesting piece of information" that Morley had, perhaps inadvertently, supplied was that Eliot's feeling about his first marriage "was one of more than remorse, it was one of guilt, and what looked like exaggerated guilt." Matthews concluded that Eliot had sought to block the publication of a biography because he wanted to keep the circumstances surrounding his first marriage private.

During the period covered by this journal, 1970–72, Valerie Eliot published her facsimile edition of *The Waste Land* and

---

5   The Matthews-Morley correspondence is found in the Matthews Papers, Series 3: Correspondence 1931–1990, Morley Frank, Box 30, Folder 21.

Robert Sencourt's much-maligned *T. S. Eliot: A Memoir* also came out. Matthews details his extensive correspondence about both books. In January 1971, the BBC released *Omnibus Presents: The Mysterious Mr Eliot* with this description: "[T. S. Eliot] received more honours in his lifetime than any other writer, but to most people almost nothing is known of his life and personality; he seems a mystery."

At times, Matthews feared he would never be able to complete his project. As an outlet, he began to keep a journal detailing his progress and the challenges he encountered, interleaved with letters and notes. If he never published the book, perhaps he could still recount the story of trying to write it. But ultimately Matthews delivered his biography, *Great Tom: Notes Towards the Definition of T. S. Eliot*, in 1973. He said he chose the subtitle to acknowledge "that this will not be the last word on the subject."

And indeed it wasn't. In the half century since then, Eliot's poems, prose and letters have been compiled and published in multiple volumes, and the poet has been the subject of several more biographies, including those written by Peter Ackroyd, Lyndall Gordon and Robert Crawford.

Matthews died in 1991 at the age of 90. In 2008, his literary executors donated his papers to Princeton University, where Matthews and his son had been undergraduates. When Princeton announced the acquisition in January 2009, Don Skemer, then curator of manuscripts for the Department of Rare Books and Special Collections, said, "The library is particularly pleased to have the Matthews Papers because they complement our excellent holdings on modern literature and publishing history, but also contain some interesting files pertaining to American politics during the Cold War."[6]

---

6 "Library Acquires Papers of Former *TIME* Editor," https://www.princeton.edu/news/2009/01/13/library-acquires-papers-former-time-editor (retrieved February 8, 2022).

Two boxes related specifically to Matthews's research on his book, in addition to folders of correspondence with Eliot's contemporaries, archivists, and publishers.[7] But in Eliot scholarly circles, the papers went unnoticed. This book, *Writing Great Tom*, is a draft manuscript, which I found in one of the folders. It is reprinted with permission of Matthews's executors.

In the Acknowledgements in *Great Tom*, Matthews thanked Mrs. Eliot for at least answering his letters when others did not. But privately, he used this journal as an outlet for all the anger and frustration he was experiencing. He concluded, "I found that not every man's hand was against me—or woman's either. The list of those who were helpful to me took up several printed pages in my book. But in general the Eliot family and close friends, and what I might call the Eliot Establishment, closed ranks and would have nothing to do with me."

Matthews thought he made two important discoveries in the course of his research. He was the first biographer to access the papers of Eliot's first wife, Vivien Haigh-Wood,[8] at the Bodleian Library. He also learned about Emily Hale.

In June 1972, a year before his contractual deadline, he reported to another archivist that Valerie Eliot remained "adamant" about restricting his access to her husband's papers, but recorded that he would be able to review Vivien's: "It took me two years to get access to those papers of Vivien Eliot's at the Bodleian. I tried everything I could think of—short of burglary." The archivists at the Bodleian Library had told him they were "of no interest." Matthews later observed that the librarians had not given the papers "the time nor the careful reading that I did," for

---

7 Finding Aid, T. S. Matthews Papers, 1910–1971 (mostly 1940–1991), Princeton University Library https://findingaids.princeton.edu/catalog/C1131, retrieved February 7, 2022.

8 In the foreword, this author has followed the style of The Letters of T. S. Eliot in spelling Vivien's name.

he ultimately turned up something that was of interest: "Vivien's neurotic but moving description of her final meeting with TSE" and "some tantalizing photographs. . . ."

He had a number of meetings with Maurice Haigh-Wood, Vivien's brother, gathering details about Vivien herself as well as about Eliot's first marriage, which had ended decades earlier.

As for Hale, Matthews seemed to ignore several early tips he received about the letters she had donated to Princeton. Five months after Princeton Archivist William Dix mentioned the number of embargoed letters, Matthews wrote back: "Do you really mean 1,000—or was that a slip of the typewriter for 100?" The archivist assured him it was no typo.[9]

As he worked on the book, Matthews created two handwritten lists of "awkward questions" about Eliot that his book would have to address. The poet's relationship with Hale was one of them. After he published his biography, Matthews wrote that in Hale's case, "I had to rely entirely on the evidence and hearsay of her friends, so the picture I gradually formed of her could not be very satisfactory—to me or to them either."

In his Acknowledgements, Matthews did not name all of the people who helped him, presumably because they, too, were navigating their own relationships with Valerie Eliot.

One was Mary Trevelyan. Biographer Christopher Sykes informed Matthews that Trevelyan was "a lady who had been much disappointed by Eliot's marriage to Valerie." When Matthews finally met Trevelyan, he wrote in his notes, "I was a little startled by her appearance; she might have been Michael Hordern[10] in women's clothes. Very hearty, firm handshake, bonhomme or faux bonhomme. She reminded me of a line of

---

9 The Matthews-Dix correspondence is found in the Matthews Papers, Series 3: Correspondence 1931–1990, Dix, William S., Box 19, Folder 17. Matthews's Boston-based financial advisers served as the executors of Hale's estate, and told him about her gift in 1970.
10 Hordern (1911–1995) was a well-known British actor.

Eliot's—or rather one he lifted—'I would meet you upon this honestly.'"

After a meeting with Trevelyan, Matthews wrote a memo for himself, noting that his wife thought Trevelyan was "wacky," and that he was "reasonably sure she is a most unreliable witness," because she reported that John Hayward never said "one word against Eliot after being cruelly abandoned." But away from "unpleasant facts," Matthews thought she was more credible. "I think TSE was a very sensitive and complicated person whose 'friends' were less complicated—and less fundamentally tough," he observed in his notes.[11]

Trevelyan shared whiskies with Matthews, and in the process, they grew closer. Matthews recalled that she spoke of Eliot "with great fondness, said that they were very good friends for twenty years, and that 'he often sat in that chair where you're sitting.'"

Trevelyan told Matthews that she had written a memoir about her relationship with Eliot, and that it was now in the hands of Dame Helen Gardner, the Eliot scholar, "whose orders I'm taking." The journal, Matthews later noted, contained more than 100 letters from Eliot, "long and funny, some of them." Trevelyan said she had shown the document to Mrs. Eliot, "who, after much thought and even praying about it," told her "she was against any more books on TSE 'just at present'; that a certain amount of time should pass to let nasty rumors (about TSE being a homo and a hypochondriac) die down." Trevelyan strongly disputed insinuations that Eliot was a homosexual, but said he was, in fact, "a hypochondriacal old gentleman."

Late in his research Matthews persuaded Trevelyan to let him read her memoir, promising not to quote from it. In notes he captured afterwards, he wrote, "I am sure, however, that Mary

---

11 "Notes of a Conversation with Mary Trevelyan at Cavendish Hall, September 2, 1972," Matthews Papers, Series 5a, Subject Files, Subject Files Fo-W, 1934–74, Box 43, Folder 7, Other Women Folder.

should stick to her guns and refuse to let Valerie cannibalize her Journal to piece out TSE's selection of letters. . . . The Journal should be brought out by itself—but I can't see Valerie ever giving her permission to publish; so I fear Mary's only recourse is to do as she has threatened, and consign the whole thing to the archives of the Oxford Press, to be exhumed after we are all in the grave."[12]

After reading the letters Eliot had written to Trevelyan, Matthews observed that they had made Eliot seem "roundly human." The journal provided "the only evidence I've seen that this side of him existed—and was a constant side of him. The letters to her prattle: they're also clever and funny and easy."[13]

When Matthews later asked Trevelyan if he could use an anecdote about Eliot's childhood from one of the letters, she said no, explaining that she still did not have permission to use them. Matthews and Trevelyan continued to commiserate about what they referred to as "Topic A," namely Valerie's control over Eliot's letters.[14]

Trevelyan told Matthews that she thought she and Hayward were "perhaps the only real friends" Eliot had had. Although she had twice proposed marriage to Eliot, she told the biographer that "'he was unmarriageable' (after he became 'grand'): selfish, hypochondriacal ('and death—well, that's all through his poems'); couldn't take criticism." After capturing Trevelyan's words, Matthews wrote to himself: "For one who was as fond of him as she says she was, this is pretty strong stuff."[15]

---

12 "After reading Mary Trevelyan's Journal, Nov. 28, 1972," Other Women Folder. Trevelyan's memoir, *The Pope of Russell Square*, was eventually published in 2022, incorporated into *Mary and Mr. Eliot: A Sort of Love Story*, co-authored by Erica Wagner.
13 "After reading Mary Trevelyan's Journal, Nov. 28, 1972," Other Women Folder.
14 The Trevelyan correspondence is found in the Matthews Papers, Series 3: Correspondence 1931–1990, Trevelyan, Mary, 1971–1974, Box 37, Folder 9.
15 "After reading Mary Trevelyan's Journal, Nov. 28, 1972."

Trevelyan told Matthews that she knew about Emily Hale, and that Eliot "dreaded his last meeting with her." But she was surprised to learn from him that Hale had "stashed" more than one thousand letters in the Princeton Library.

In his Acknowledgements, Matthews also did not credit Barbie Sturtevant, an old friend who was Eleanor Hinkley's niece and Eliot's second cousin. Matthews wrote her in June 1970, asking if she would share her memories of her relative. Sturtevant responded with what Matthews told her was a "marvellous, more-than-hoped-for, couldn't-be-more-helpful letter." She recalled visiting Eliot and Vivien in London in 1922 when she was twelve, and that Vivien had seemed fragile and mysterious, and somewhat scary to a child of that age. Sturtevant also wrote about later meetings with Eliot when he was visiting Cambridge, or traveling there with Valerie in his final years.

Matthews hoped to be able to interview Eleanor Hinkley, who was still living in the Cambridge home where Eliot and Hale had performed together nearly sixty years before. But by then, Valerie Eliot had told Matthews she was going to instruct Eliot's family members not to cooperate with him. (Hinkley, along with other family members and Valerie herself, did appear in the BBC documentary.) Matthews advised Sturtevant about Valerie's decree even as he struggled over whether he could ethically use the information she had already provided. Sturtevant later worried that Valerie might have learned that she had spoken with Matthews, but he assured Sturtevant that he had protected her.

Behind his polite letters, Matthews's narrative and his correspondence with his editor provide a franker view of the challenges he faced and his true feelings about those he was trying to interview.

One person Matthews did acknowledge was Dorothy Elsmith, a longtime confidante of Hale's who provided Hale and Eliot with a private place to meet when Eliot came to the States. But Matthews connected with Elsmith late in his research, and much of the information she provided ended up in his files but not in his book. That included the eulogy delivered at Hale's funeral in October 1969, just a few months before Matthews began his work. The minister recalled that Hale had attended church the week before she died, and had been expected to attend the morning of her death. Hale also performed in *My Fair Lady* in the spring of 1968 and took a cruise to South America later that summer, all facts that seem to contradict the cited memories of Sally Foss, a Hale student who recounted, at age ninety-six, that Hale had been bedridden at the Colonial Inn in Concord for the final two years of her life and didn't travel.[16]

Matthews wrote that not long after Eliot died, Mrs. Eliot visited Hale, but he provided no further details to back up that story. When the Eliot Estate published Eliot's letters to Hale online in January 2023, it included two letters that Hale sent Valerie in 1966 and 1968, confirming that Hale reached out to her in November 1966 at Hinkley's urging: "There is no question that Emily has changed and has now a real fear of what the literary hounds would do if they caught the scent! I suggested that she write to you. And at least start a conventional acquaintance and perhaps get to know each other. Not to know her is in itself a kind of provocation to curiosity, for those who are perpetually on the watch for gossip. But, my dear, I am not trying to force you into anything that is alien to you. I am only suggesting that the time is ripe for it and that there could be practical advantages to it."

They later met in person, presumably in 1968 when Valerie made a trip to the United States to inspect the original manuscript of *The Waste Land* at the New York Public Library.[17]

---

16 Susan Stewart and Joshua Kotin, "A Conversation with Sally Foss about Emily Hale, *Time Present: The Newsletter of the International T. S. Eliot Society*, Spring 2020, Number 100, 23. Robert Crawford cites the Foss interview in his biography *Eliot After The Waste Land* (London: Penguin Random House, 2022), 484.
17 Emily Hale to Valerie, November 6, 1966 and November [?], 1968, The Eliot-Hale Letters, www.tseliot.com.

The Princeton archives show that when Matthews interviewed Elsmith, he captured notes that read: "E. H. is a very clever mimic—marvellous sense of humor (after meeting Valerie gave Mrs. Elsmith an uproarious imitation—which she won't describe)."[18]

The editor in Matthews could not resist sending letters to Mrs. Eliot, Faber and Faber executive Peter du Sautoy and biographer Peter Ackroyd, pointing out typographical and other errors in the books they had written, edited or published. But once again those polite letters masked Matthews's anger, particularly after Valerie published the facsimile edition of *The Waste Land*, detailed editing changes that others had made to the work. Matthews believed her publication flouted even more explicit instructions that Eliot had left behind regarding future publication.[19]

Thus the Matthews papers provide new details about Eliot's life and, at a minimum, the sources of some stories and anecdotes recounted in his book. And this, Matthews's engaging story about writing *Great Tom*, chronicles his side of his battles with Mrs. Eliot, his candid views of persons he interviewed, his battles with archivists at Harvard, the University of Texas, and Oxford, and the dilemmas he faced as a journalist/biographer.

Great Tom was an imperfect and incomplete book, as its author, some reviewers, and later scholars have acknowledged. But fifty years later, the Matthews papers still offer, perhaps surprisingly, new nuggets of information about Eliot's story and the stories of key people in his life. They also provide some broader lessons for all who wrestle with the challenges of contemporary biography.

---

18 Matthews Papers, Elsmith Correspondence Folder.
19 These letters are found in the Matthews Correspondence series, the folders for Valerie Eliot, Peter Du Sautoy, and Peter Ackroyd.

EDITOR'S NOTE

Writing Great Tom comprises material written by T. S. Matthews and found in 2021 by Sara Fitzgerald among his papers at Princeton University. The material was in a single folder, and consists of a typed journal and additional notes as well as well as the text of what seems to have been meant as a speech. The folder also contained duplicate pages, which we have removed. The hundreds of pages had been rearranged and renumbered more than once, but we were able to piece them together, and place stray pages, in what we think is a clear and logical narrative. We will be grateful to readers who contact us if they note errors.

We have added only a few footnotes as this is not intended to be a scholarly annotated edition. Obvious misspellings and minor errors have been silently corrected, but we have retained Matthews's frequent use of English spellings and his frequent capitalization. The many letters Matthews quotes have been indented for easy reading (in the original, they were quoted within his typed diary). The material has been logically arranged, but nothing has been removed, added, or changed. In cases where Matthews had begun editing by crossing out words or passages, we have included the text as he first typed it. Handwritten additions have been silently added to the text. Matthews occasionally included several versions of the same passage. If there are no substantive differences, the texts have been merged or the less complete one deleted.

WRITING GREAT TOM
T. S. Eliot & the Keepers of the Flame

INTRODUCTION:
LIVING A DETECTIVE STORY

I believe that T. S. ELIOT was a great poet and a good man. The two don't necessarily go together. In fact, we can cite many cases of poets in whom greatness of accomplishments meet and sweetness of nature have seemed far apart – in the 17th century, for example, JOHN MILTON, in the 20th century ROBERT FROST.

The outline of TSE's life is well known – we all know that he was born in America, in St. Louis, Missouri (wherever that is),[20] that he came to England as a young man and worked in a London bank and wore a bowler and carried a rolled umbrella; that he wrote some rather arresting verse about a hippopotamus and the Church, and another about a lady of easy virtue named GRISHKIN,[21] and then a whopping long poem called The Waste Land, very gloomy but full of quotations and quotable lines; that he was awarded the Nobel Prize for Literature and also the Order of Merit; that he wrote another long poem, very deep stuff, called Four Quartets, and that he died a few years ago (actually it was in 1965). And that his

---

20 Because T. S. Matthews was born in Cincinnati, Ohio, and lived in the United States for his first fifty years, he certainly knew where St. Louis was located. This remark, and others, suggest this was aimed at a British audience. This portion of the document reads like a speech that Matthews may have delivered.
21 Grishkin appears in the 1920 Eliot poem "Whispers of Immortality."

fame is not confined to Britain and the United States: his poems have been translated into 39 languages – and this is amazing, when you come to think of it. How can lines like:

> The young are red and pustular
> Clutching piaculative pence

be rendered in Japanese, for example? Or how these lines lend themselves to Hungarian?

> Gull against the wind, in the windy straits
> Of Belle Isle, or running on the Horn.
> White feathers in the snow, The Gulf claims,
> And an old man driven by the Trades
> To a sleepy corner.

(Philip Sidney: A tale which holdeth children from play, and old men from the chimney corner.)

But many details of TSE's life remain unknown, at least to the public. It <u>is</u> generally known that he married twice, but most people have never heard of EMILY HALE, the woman with whom he had a lifelong friendship and who hoped to marry him. And there are other questions: what were the circumstances under which he married his first wife, VIVIENNE; and why were neither his family nor hers invited to the wedding? Why did he leave a memorandum with his will enjoining his literary executor (his second wife, VALERIE) to give no encouragement or help to anyone who wanted to write his biography? The answer to that last question is, I think, fairly obvious: he wanted to bury, for as long as possible, the record of his agonizing first marriage.

One of the prices a man pays for greatness (the laurel wreath bestowed on him by his fellow men) is loss of privacy. His fellow men demand to know – they seem to think they have right to know – all there is to know about him. And this demand is perhaps not altogether based on merely idle or mischievous curiosity. As the biographer of Joyce and Yeats, PROFESSOR RICHARD ELLMANN, says: "The effort to know another person as well as we know a character in fiction, and better than we know ourselves, is not frivolous. It may even be, for reader as for writer, an essential part of experience. (Foreword of my book, Great Tom): "The more that human beings can learn about other human beings, this side of nausea, the better. There is more to learn than we can take in, and not much in time in which to learn it. And from whom should we learn but from those who – no matter what they think of themselves – act, ponder, speak or write in ways we can all admire but which few of us can hope to emulate? TSE was of that kidney."

TSE himself, when he was 68, said in a public lecture, later collected in a book:

> I do not suggest that the personality and the private life of a dead poet constitute sacred ground on which the psychologist must not tread. The scientist must be at liberty to study such material as his curiosity leads him to investigate, as long as the victim is dead and the law of libel cannot be invoked to stop him. Nor is there any reason why biographies of poets should not be written. They are very useful. Any critic seriously concerned with a man's work should be expected to know something about the man's life.

I am not a biographer by trade, and the only biography I have written unless you include an autobiography which I don't think you should, is my life of ELIOT, Great Tom. The biography was written on commission – i.e., a publisher suggested that I write it. It would never, I confess, have occurred to me to write it on my own hook. It took me three years, and I could happily and profitably have spent longer.

Or perhaps I should never have written it. A good many people seem to be of that opinion, to judge by some of the reviews. A great many books are not reviewed at all, so maybe

6 WRITING GREAT TOM

I can count myself fortunate that Great Tom was so widely reviewed on both sides of the Atlantic; but some of the things that were said about it were not calculated to make an author purr with pleasure. Here are a few:

"... a dull and obtuse book."

"... persistence in treating what is complex and large as if it were simple and insignificant."

"This book is so empty of real information, so ill-organized, so badly documented, so vulgar in its language and proposal, so shabby in its homilies and deductions as to arouse rage..."

"... may prove a rich source for collectors of contemporary nonsense."

Those brickbats were thrown from my own country, America. Some of the bouquets from this side were hurled with even greater force:

"Innuendo carefully proffered and carefully withdrawn, sneers accompanied by ostensibly balancing praise, these distasteful adroitnesses are well in evidence..." (This from a review by a man who had written a book on The Impulse to Dominate.)[22]

"... stark, staring silliness ... full-bloodedly inept... a classic of incongruity."

---

22 D. W. Harding, a British psychologist and literary critic, was the author of *The Impulse to Dominate*. He contributed to *The New York Review of Books*, among other publications.

"The level of the writing seldom rises above competent journalism and frequently descends to the cute vulgarity that pervades <u>TIME</u>, of which Mr. Matthews was once the editor."

Perhaps one or two of you may have read my book, and perhaps you may agree with the judgments I have just cited. Obviously I don't, or I should not now be standing before you with my throat uncut. I've done a good deal of book-reviewing myself, in my day, and I know the rhadamanthine feeling of pointing at some guilty wretch who has written a bad book or one of which I disapproved and ordering him, in no uncertain terms, to go straightway to hell. He might demur, but of course he had to go. When you are reviewing someone else's book it is sometimes hard not to have such delusions of grandeur. I confess I have occasionally suffered from them.

But after I had written my first book (that was more than 40 years ago) I realized what a labor it is to write even a bad book (and I didn't think that first one of mine was much better than that). Thereafter I tried to remember that this fact when I held in my hands the battered progeny of someone else's blood, sweat and tears. It was a state of grace, alas, that I found difficult to maintain. Nevertheless, its occasional visitation left me with a certain amount of sympathy for most writers, even including book-reviewers. No doubt some of you here tonight have written books, perhaps several, perhaps many; but it is on the supposition that most of you have not that I venture to tell you something – there is not time enough in one evening to tell you everything luckily for you, of what it was like to write a biography of T. S. ELIOT.

I admired ELIOT greatly, and knew him slightly – we met, sometimes informally, perhaps a dozen times in the 20 or 25 years of our acquaintance. I had published an interview with him in an American magazine, and an article about him in another. As I say in the foreword to <u>Great Tom</u>, he "treated me with the same tender but formal solicitude he showed in all such encounters. Mine was an outsider's acquaintance; we could not be called friends. When we met, however, he remembered or almost remembered who I was. I think I could be listed among his not quite anonymous admirers."

When the New York publisher asked me to write ELIOT's life I was surprised but rather pleased. I replied by cable that it was an odd but appealing notion, and asked what MRS. ELIOT would say and whether she would let me see her husband's unpublished papers.

MRS. ELIOT's letter, of which they sent me a copy, stated flatly that she will not give the slightest encouragement or help with the proposed biography because her husband had forbidden such a thing. In time, she added, his biography must be written, but she would not assist any such project. Nonetheless, she sent her good wishes.

For reasons which I still fail to understand, the publisher found this letter "most encouraging." I did not, but I had been thinking over the proposal and by this time had become quite interested in it.

At this point I went to hospital for over two months, but when I was out the publisher sent me a contract and I signed it. By the terms of the contract I had three years in which to deliver the finished manuscript.

I wrote to MRS. ELIOT on my own hook and got a reply very similar to the one she had sent to the publishers. She remembered having met me two or three times, and said she had pleasant memories of those occasions. I wrote to her a second time, asking if she would be willing to see me when I was well enough to come to London; and I thought we might save time and trouble if she could then tell me herself viva voce, just which collections of papers were out of bounds.

She wrote back, still very pleasant, but quite firm, saying that she saw no useful purpose in seeing me again, that all papers were out of bounds and that if we did meet I wouldn't be able to help "trying to press her." She also added that ELIOT's family were with her in this and would give me no help.

By this time I was sufficiently interested to want to go further and see whether there was not enough material to make a decent book about ELIOT without being allowed to use the forbidden papers. I knew that a great deal had been written on the subject; I was told that there were more than a thousand books in the British Museum on ELIOT and his works. I couldn't possible read all of these in the two years I had allotted myself for doing the research, but I figured I could read enough of them – say two hundred – to find out whether or not there was enough there for a book.

So I began to make lists of people to see, books to read, places to go and questions to ask. I was not at all methodical about this at first, and I wasn't really up to doing very much for several months, while I was convalescing.

* * *

The next three years were like living a detective story. Someone suggested that I keep a record of it, and then, if I found it impossible to write the ELIOT biography, I would have a book showing why it had been impossible – so I tried to keep such a record. I shall not inflict much of it on you this evening, but I shall read you a few bits – and also try to tell you something of two discoveries that I found very interesting: VIVIENNE ELIOT's papers – and EMILY HALE.

I learned about VIVIENNE ELIOT's papers from reading a copy of her will, in which she left them all to the Bodleian Library at Oxford. And I discovered EMILY HALE quite by accident, through a friend of mine who had been one of her pupils at Smith College in Massachusetts. I thought it typical of my luck at the time that Miss Hale died just six months before I first heard of her.[23]

---

23 Hale died on October 12, 1969.

In the case of EMILY HALE, I had to rely entirely on the evidence and hearsay of her friends, so the picture I gradually formed of her could not be very satisfactory – to me or to them either, I'm afraid. Rather like an Identikit, I think they're called – one of those drawings put out by the police based on the descriptions of those who have caught a glimpse of the wanted man – or who think they have. Here's a bit of the Identikit: She spent many summers with her uncle and aunt in Chipping Camden.

T. S. ELIOT did not want his life written, and had left a memorandum attached to his will enjoining her to give no help whatever to any would-be biographer. Although this memorandum had no legal force, [VALERIE ELIOT] felt morally bound bit, and could therefore not make any of his unpublished papers available to me or to any other biographer. Perhaps this should have stopped me in my tracks, but by this time I was getting more and more interested in the idea of writing a life of ELIOT. His veto and its consequences would form a considerable obstacle but need not, I though, prevent my writing some sort of biography. The main facts of his life were known and could not be concealed: there were still surviving friends of his who might be willing to talk to me about him; in the hundreds of books that had already been written about him and his works there must be some biographical nuggets.

One scholar and authority on ELIOT whom I went to see and who was sympathetically neutral in this argument gave me some valuable advice: Read all of ELIOT's letters, he said, that you can lay your hands on; in them you will find many facts about him that have not yet found their way into print. When I started to collect material for this book I soon discovered that there were three main collections of ELIOT papers: the Houghton Library at Harvard, the University of Texas, and King's College Library, Cambridge.

The Houghton Library would not admit me without MRS. ELIOT's permission (which was of course not forthcoming); the librarian at the University of Texas sent me a list of the ELIOT papers there, indicating which ones I would be allowed to see (almost none) and agreed that it would not be worth my while to make the long trip to Texas on such a sleeveless errand.

But at King's College, Cambridge I had better luck. The librarian there, DR. A. N. L. MUNBY, was the curator of a collection of papers given to the library by ELIOT's friend JOHN HAYWARD; some of these papers were sealed off from any eyes (even including MRS. ELIOT's!) until the date when the copyright expired; but the rest I was allowed to look at. And I found another small collection of ELIOT material at Brown University, in Providence, Rhode Island.

It took me two years to get access to those papers of VIVIENNE ELIOT's at the Bodleian. I tried everything I could think of – short of burglary. I even wrote to the WARDEN of All Soul's:

> Dear Warden: I know you are not an admirer of TSE, I believe you are on the side of common sense and fair play. Also I gather you are not averse to an occasional dust-up if the casus belli seems to warrant it. Therefore, although almost a stranger to you, I am applying to you for help.
>
> Four days after posting this letter I learned from the Sunday Telegraph that the Warden was taking a sabbatical in Italy!
>
> I did finally manage to penetrate the Bodleian. With the sympathetic help of a young friend who worked for the Clarendon Press I drafted a letter to Bodley's Librarian, gently but firmly insisting on my rights as a senior member of the University and a serious researcher – and it worked!
>
> I was told by the Librarian the same story his Curator of Manuscripts had told me two years before: that he had looked over the material when it first arrived and that there was nothing in it. Perhaps

neither of these gentlemen gave Vivienne's papers the time nor the careful reading that I did. For I did find something: Vivienne's neurotic but moving description of her final meeting with TSE, some tantalizing photographs – particularly of Janes, the retired policeman who was a kind of family retainer and who acted as a watchdog for TSE during his separation from V.

I said a little earlier that I was allowed to see – though not allowed to take any notes – the original typescript of The Waste Land, at the Public Library in New York. A year after I started work on Great Tom, Valerie Eliot brought out a facsimile edition. A fascinating book, but neither its price not its subject are apt to appeal to the general public. My guess is that TSE himself would greatly have preferred an edition of one copy – or possibly two. When he sent the typescript as a present to John Quinn, the irascible New York lawyer who acted as Maecenas[24] to many painters and writers (including TSE). TSE wrote Quinn two letters about it.

So far I have barely mentioned the name of Ezra Pound, but I am sure you know about him, and know about his relation to TSE. In a sense he was TSE's discoverer: he was responsible for getting TSE's first poems published, and he was the man who edited The Waste Land by the drastic method of cutting out nearly half of it. There was no secret about this, and TSE always gave Pound credit for editing the poem; but until the facsimile Waste Land was rediscovered nobody knew just *what* Pound had cut out. Now we can see, and it is a tribute to his poetic eye and

---

24 Gaius Maecenas was a counselor to the Roman emperor Augustus and a patron of the arts.

editorial judgment that we find it easy to agree with his excisions. Or almost all.

The 50-odd lines that originally began the poem tell about a night out in some city, presumably Boston; they are no loss. (Incidentally, the original title of The Waste Land appears on that page: He Do The Police in Different Voices.)

But TSE was rather reluctant to give up the 70 lines of heroic couplets in the manner of Pope[25]. He yielded when Pound pointed out that "you cannot parody Pope unless you can write better verse than Pope – and you can't."

TSE was a shy man, and he was shy about stating his real beliefs. I think he felt himself a superior person but nevertheless a miserable sinner, perhaps a damned one: a man who lived on the agonizing rack of paradox, whose poems were almost literally made in hell. One of his perceptive Oriental critics said: "Not all of us can share Eliot's faith, but all of us can accept the poetry because every line of it was written while looking into the eyes of the demon." He tended to see life itself in terms of "the white flat face of death." Another Eliot scholar thinks that "the average church-goer...would be most disconcerted by a real glimpse into Eliot's mind. There is a savagery in that mind." "For thine is the boredom & the horror & the glory TSE's parody of a phrase in the Lord's Prayer seems to me more horrifying than Hemingway's "Our Nada who art in nada." Eliot once wrote to his friend Paul Elmer More[26], he was unable to comprehend those people who did not feel the emptiness at the core of life. He was more aware of hell than of heaven.

---

25 English poet Alexander Pope (1688–1744).
26 Paul Elmer More (1864–1937) was an American critic scholar whose works, particularly those dealing with religion, were admired by Eliot.

TSE was an odd fit for a Christian – but then, aren't most Christians?

He was certainly one of the great poets of our sad century. I have ranked him, perhaps not altogether happily, with Pope. He has not the fierce, tugging attraction of [W. B.] Yeats, nor the antic charm of [Thomas] Hardy; if it were possible to combine two such poets as [Walter Savage] Landor and [John] Donne, that hippogriff combination might resemble Eliot.

If any of you are still awake, and want to ask any questions, I'll try to answer them.

MEETINGS WITH TSE

Though I wrote two or three pieces of journalism about him, I never looked at him with the eye of a biographer.

In my diaries I find 10 meetings with TSE recorded, beginning with the evening of May 11, 1950. I recollect – or think I recollect – at least three earlier meetings.

Where and when I first saw TSE I cannot be sure. I think it was in Princeton, and perhaps the year was 1932. He did come back to the US then, for the first time in 18 years, and may have visited Princeton to give a lecture or a reading. Was it in 1932? I seem to remember a sedate reception, perhaps at the Graduate School at Princeton, perhaps with an innocuous punch or very small drinks (Prohibition ended in 1931) so drinks would have been legal then), and being formally introduced to the guest of honor by PAUL ELMER MORE. This is a faint memory, but fairly clear.[27]

Ten years later, I was in Wartime London for three months. I should like to think that I saw TSE twice during that time, but can be sure of only one occasion. That was at LADY COLEFAX's[28] house on Lord North Street, at tea. I had

---

27 On March 23, 1933, during the academic year he spent at Harvard, Eliot delivered the Spencer Trask Foundation Lecture at Princeton on the topic "The Bible and English Literature. Matthews was a member of the Princeton Class of 1922.
28 Lady Sybil Colefax (1874–1950) was an English socialite and interior decorator.

propounded this tea-party myself, as I was bored stiff with the weekly dinner at the Dorchester over which she presided and for which she always produced a rotten mangy sort of loin, and for which you (or your office) were always presented later with a bill. When I told LADY COLEFAX that I much preferred her company to the sandwiched lions at the Dorch, she responded by inviting me to Sunday lunch with a much more select company (e.g., LADY DIANA COOPER, SIR RONALD STORRS) and to tea, which was to be a tête-à-tête. Did I suggest her asking TSE?

Not in any case, there we were, the three of us, in LADY COLEFAX's little band-box of a first-floor sitting room, a cozy fire on the hearth and the blacked-out London fog outside. We formed, I felt, a most Eliotesque scene. Our conversation tinkled among the tea-cups; our remarks (even LADY COLEFAX's) verged on the prim. I watched TSE with fascination. He seemed to me to be holding himself together, almost as if he were balanced on the edge of the sofa, and that if he lowered his carefully held cup without rearranging his carefully held feet (but of course he did) he might fall over. I though how deracinated he seemed: how non-English (and how non-American) his polite accents were, how deeply he seemed to hold himself in, how neatly he was dressed and with what propriety his hair was combed. Did he seem to LADY COLEFAX as uprooted, as outlandish, as he seemed to me? And how did he appear to himself? Most Americans, I thought, would consider him quite anglicized; but few Englishmen would mistake him for one of themselves.

Into the midst of this careful and on the whole most agreeable tea party and smashing it to bits like a clumsy and well-meaning big dog, bounded the beaming and complacent, the ruddy and rotund figure of HAROLD NICOLSON.[29] I found it a most

---

29 Harold Nicolson (1886–1968) was a British diplomat and husband of Vita Sackville-West.

unwelcome interruption. Evidently not so, however, to our
hostess, who hailed the intruder with enthusiasm. NICOLSON,
fresh from the House of Commons, was full of himself, as he
always was, bursting with political gossip, hot off the griddle
and ahead of the papers and the BBC The next half-hour was a
whooping, giggling monologue, bristling with first names and
inside-stuff lingo, interspersed with screams of delight and
encouragement from LADY COLEFAX. All this club talk was of no
interest whatever to me, and quite incomprehensible; by his
complete absence of expression and utter silence, I gathered
that MR. ELIOT felt much the same way. Our fragile tea-party
lay in fragments on the sitting-room carpet; as soon as we
decently could we took our separate leaves.

Where was our next encounter? In Princeton again? I can't
be certain, but I have an idea that it was. Perhaps during the
few months when TSE was at the Institute for Advanced Study,
finishing The Cocktail Party. That must have been in 1948.
My memories of this occasion are so dim that it may not have
happened at all.

May 11, 1950 was an ELIOT evening I remember well.
It was at 20 Chapel Street in London. I was invited there
to dinner; ELIOT and his friend JOHN HAYWARD would come
in afterwards. Before they arrived our host told me that
HAYWARD was a cripple, confined to his wheel chair, which we
should have to manhandle out of the taxi and up the stairs to
the living room. This would need four men: the taxi driver,
ELIOT, DOZIER, and myself. And that's the way it was. HAYWARD
gave the orders, like a hulking, overweight coxswain, and
we heaved and pulled accordingly. On the half-landing he
made us stop and rest; he was a heavy load. By the time we got
him ensconced in the living room we were puffed, but he was
talking sixteen to the dozen.

His face was heavy and oblong, the face of a caustic clown;
his eyebrows nearly met, and behind his horn-rimmed spectacles
his eyes moved watchfully. His lips were gross, almost swollen
(an effect of his disease) and hung open, giving him a voluptuous

look. His voice was harsh. He was adept at raising a laugh, usually at someone else's expense.

For some time ELIOT sat silent, smiling benignantly, with an expression of vague good will. He and HAYWARD had evidently dined well; the effect had been to make him as mum as HAYWARD was talkative. This didn't suit HAYWARD's book: he wanted to show ELIOT off, to "produce" him, and he tried again and again to get ELIOT going, who just sat smiling gently, apparently unable or unwilling to say a word. But at last HAYWARD drew him. The subject of SHERLOCK HOLMES did the trick. HAYWARD averred that ELIOT knew these stories so well that he could recite whole paragraphs from memory; he urged ELIOT to give us a sample.

And ELIOT finally complied. In a soft voice, almost as if to himself, he recited a passage from one of the Sherlock HOLMES stories: "It was some time before the health of my friend, MR. SHERLOCK HOLMES, recovered from the strain caused by his immense exertions in the spring of '87 . . . at a time when Europe was ringing with his name, and when his room was literally ankle-deep with congratulatory telegrams, I found him a prey to the blackest depression." [30]

That broke the log-jam; ELIOT went on to quote a passage from another HOLMES story, The Retired Colourman, in which WATSON describes the site of a crime: "You know that particular quarter, the monotonous brick streets, the weary suburban highways. Right in the middle of them, a little island of ancient culture and comfort, lies this old home, surrounded by a high sun-baked wall mottled with lichens and topped with moss, the sort of wall. . ."

"Cut out the poetry, WATSON," said HOLMES severely. "I note that it was a high brick wall."

"Cut out the poetry," ELIOT murmured, again. "That's what I've been trying to do all my life."

---

[30] The quote is from the Arthur Conan Doyle story "The Adventure of the Reigate Squire."

In December of that same year--if I have the date and the occasion, I saw ELIOT again, this meeting in New York, at the Central Park South apartment of a couple (could it have been the E. MCKNIGHT KAUFFERS?)[31] who were intimate friend of ELIOT's. I was then on leave from TIME, working on their experimental project for a little magazine, and I wanted to ask ELIOT some questions about the Criterion, whose life had ended in 1939, after a run of nearly 19 years.

Though the appointment was supposed to have been made by somebody on TIME, when I showed up at the Central Park South apartment there were several other people there, but no ELIOT. My hostess offered me a drink, which I stiffly refused (I was on the wagon at the time, which didn't improve my temper). There were three or four other people there, a couple of them from Life, and all waiting for ELIOT; but they were all apparently friends of his; nobody was there on business except me. ELIOT appeared, was warmly but casually greeted by his friends, and settled down with them by the fire, with a drink in his hand. I grimly waited for these preliminaries to be over, and for ELIOT to nod to me and lead the way to another room, where we could have our talk. When the drink in his hand was replaced by a second, and he showed no signs of emerging from his relaxed posture, I got my hostess into the pantry and inquired with some asperity when was I going to have my interview. She knew nothing about it, but went and fetched ELIOT. He too had heard nothing about an appointment, but was all apologies and kindly sympathy; we made an engagement to meet for coffee at the Plaza next morning, and I left.

Next morning, strictly business, we sat at a table for two in a window of the dining room in the Plaza, looking out

---

31   E. McKnight Kauffer (1890–1954) was an American artist and graphic designer who provided illustrations for some of Eliot's published poems. His wife was interior decorator Marion Dorn (1896–1964). The Kauffers moved back to New York at the start of World War II.

on 59th Street, I recall ELIOT's lean and mournful figure opposite me. We talked of little magazines. He thought that a literary paper should, ideally, support itself; but he cited some of the difficulties. When questioned, he admitted that the circulation of the <u>Criterion</u> was 900, at its peak. He was not proud of that fact.

Our next meeting was in London, the following spring. As I remember it, I went to tea at HAYWARD's invitation, in the flat he shared with ELIOT. When tea was brought in, ELIOT also appeared. There was a cat as well; possibly more than one. As before, HAYWARD did most of the talking; and as before his harsh and self-consciously clever remarks made a disagreeable effect on me. This time, as there were no ladies present, he indulged a scatological fancy which was obviously one of his gross familiars, and which I found, coming from one of his appearance and in his situation, equally repellent. ELIOT's benign, gently smiling, almost wordless presence soothed my irritation, but seemed to have an encouraging effect, like the flame under a singing tea-kettle, on the blubber-mouthed obscenities of my host. HAYWARD lately had been acting as one of the judges in a poetry contest with an enormous number of entries, many of whose inanities and unintentionally scabrous phrases had struck in his retentive memory.

Though I should have been warned off by this exhibition of HAYWARD's critical prowess, I wasn't; and after "his lodger" – as HAYWARD liked to refer to ELIOT – had left the room, I handed him a sheaf of my own verses for his criticism and comments. What I really hoped for, of course, was that HAYWARD would be sufficiently struck by them to show them to ELIOT – but this didn't happen. When I next saw HAYWARD, some ten days later, at a cocktail party I have at the Connaught, he gravely pointed out to me the primary (I might almost say "the nursery") rules of scansion and rhyme, and cited numerous instances – all of them quite deliberate on my part – when I had failed to obey these childish laws. I thank him and privately cursed myself for being such a fool as to imagine that he might be of any help.

It may well be that I have telescoped two occasions at Cheyne Walk into one, or mixed them up; for the next diary entry, for February 14, 1953, has the notation 4.30, which is tea-time; whereas the 1951 date is for 3.15. Ay any rate, I went there twice, and think I saw ELIOT on both occasion. The general aspect of this flat, its air of suburban steam-heated comfort, was a disappointment to me; it seemed to me too padded and warm, out of keeping with the dwelling of a poet.

Three days later, on February 17, I went to a luncheon-party at Gunter's (then at the top of Curzon Street)[32] given by LADY PENTLAND,[33] an affair of about a dozen people, one of them ELIOT. I am sure that we exchanged politeness, and that they were nothings.

On November 16, 1953, my diary records that I went to ELIOT's office, in the rather ramshackle corner building, that housed Faber & Faber in Russell Square. As I recall it, his office was on the top floor, or at any rate several flights up, and I don't remember any lift. His office was small and cramped, crowded with books and manuscripts. And made a cramped impression. I think I must have been seeing him about a piece I was to write for <u>Life</u>, timed to coincide with the New York opening of his play, <u>The Confidential Clerk</u>. As always, he was kindness itself, attentive and almost differential. I was sure he didn't think much of <u>Life</u> (neither did I), but he gave no inkling of it. He offered me a cup of tea, which I accepted: milk, but no sugar. Was this when I first met his future wife, VALERIE? I vaguely remember a secretary, a rather large young woman. VALERIE was his secretary for seven years before they married.

After this there is a lapse of nearly five years: the next entry in my diary about TSE is dated March 18, 1958. He and

---

32 Gunter's Tea Shop.
33 Marjorie Sinclair, Baroness Pentland (1880–1970).

VALERIE had been married then not much over a year. I saw them in ROSAMOND LEHMANN's[34] flat off Eaton Square; I think they had been having dinner there, and my wife and I came in afterwards.[35] There were other people there, of whom I think I remember the WHITNEYS and LEON EDEL, the biographer of HENRY JAMES. ELIOT was now 70, and a world figure, full of honors; but his behavior was still shy and subdued – except with VALERIE. In spite of the fact that they were far from being alone, they held hands and gazed tenderly at each other, while ELIOT had his hand around her ample shoulders or patted her biceps. Everyone pretended to take no notice, but it was a spectacle, pathetic, delightful or ridiculous, according to the eye of the beholder.

My diary for June 9, 1958 says "Call ELIOT – Wed. or Thurs. morning?" and for the next day: "8 – ELIOT's to dinner." I haven't the slightest recollection of this event. Might it be that both these entries refer to TSE's distant cousin, ALEXANDER ELIOT, who had worked with me on TIME as its Art editor? It might indeed. And yet... On June 12 my diary has this entry: "12 – ELIOT" (with a question mark, crossed out – which means that the meeting, tentatively arranged, did occur). And I do remember – or think I do! – being in his office at Faber & Faber's on at least two occasions, of which this would have been the second. It was at about this time that I was writing an article about him for the New York Times Magazine, and with his unfailing patience he consented to an interview – though it must have been the thousand-&-first. Again I have a memory of that cup of unsugared tea, though this time it must have been a different secretary who brought it.

My last meeting with ELIOT was on May 25, 1960 – five years before he died. The ELIOTs had invited my wife and me

---

34 Rosamond Lehmann (1901–1990) was the author of provocative novels and a member of the Bloomsbury set.
35 When Matthews wrote Valerie Eliot on May 30, 1957, asking to meet with her, he referenced this evening. (Matthews Papers, Valerie Eliot Correspondence Folder.)

to dinner at their Kensington flat, where MRS. ELIOT still lives. It was a small party: the only other guest was JOHN LEHMANN, ROSAMOND's brother, a literary man about town and a bald pederast whom I found repulsive but who was on first-name terms with the ELIOTS - as I most decidedly was not. I remember nothing remarkable about the dinner, nor about the evening, which produced the predictable literary small talk, except that my wife and I, by a mutual meeting of eyes, agreed that we wanted to cut it short, and took our leave at an early hour, just barely consonant with politeness, over the regretful protests of both the ELIOTS. The inclination to cut short the evening was reinforced not only by our dislike of EDWARD LEHMAN but by our embarrassment at the ELIOTS' connubial carryings-on, which here, in the fastness of their own home, they obviously felt freer to indulge.

1970

I have now been at this job for about six months and I have reached the point where I think I should keep a daily log of my activities. I can't go back and pick up all the lost days in the past six months, but there may be a few individual days I can pick out, and I will date them. At present, I think the best thing I can do is to try to summarize the present situation, and try to map out in general where I am and where I'm going from here.

The records of what I have accomplished so far is not very impressive. Perhaps twenty or so books read; about the same number of people seen; one very brief and superficial trip to America; a pilgrimage to the places mentioned in Four Quartets: East Coker, Burnt Norton, The Dry Salvages, (where I photographed the wrong rocks), and Little Gidding. I keep a copy of all correspondence, which so far I have managed to do myself; I have a card index of the books I have read which will presumably go into the bibliography;[36] and I have a file of sorts which is not very satisfactory, where I put all kinds of material that I get out of books and periodicals, and so on.

---

36 Matthews's book included a bibliography listing nearly 70 books, including collections of Eliot's poetry.

In the first few months, tales emerged. One was that there was certainly a demand for such a book. Since signing my contract with Harper & Row, or rather, since a form letter which I sent out to various newspapers and literary periodicals, some of whom printed it, I was approached by 11 publishers, five in America and six in London, all showing considerable interest, and some making an outright offer to publish the book.

Another thing is the emotion this projected life ELIOT generates. Some of my own friends have written to me, urging me not to go on with it, saying things like: "Peace to his ashes. If he didn't want his life written, why write one?" People seem to be passionately engaged – at least on his side. I am engaged, and on the other side, but I hope not passionately. So far, I sympathize with ELIOT, although I think he was wrong in this instance.

I think one of the main reasons, for ELIOT's attempt to prevent – or postpone as long as possible – the writing of his life, was his first, tragically unhappy marriage, to VIVIENNE HAIGH-WOOD. And he wanted to protect not only her but himself. She was described in a footnote, I think, in HOLROYD's Life of Lytton Strachey as 'an ether drinker'.[37] Very little is generally known about her and I am discovering little bits and pieces that are very tantalizing. The fact of their marriage is known, and the date – June, 1915. The marriage apparently broke up in 1932, when he went to America for the first time in eighteen years, and stayed for quite a long time; when he came back to England he did not go back to her. Sometime thereafter she became ill and went to a mental hospital, where she died in 1947. The only photographs of her I had seen was reproduced by the Sunday Times Colour Supplement and also by the BBC, although I think the BBC cropped VIVIENNE out of the picture. It was obviously taken

---

37 British author Michael Holroyd published his two-volume work, *Lytton Strachey: A Critical Biography,* in 1967–68.

on a weekend with LEONARD and VIRGINIA WOOLF, and LEONARD WOOLF must <u>have taken the photograph because he wasn't in the picture</u>.

MRS. ST. JOHN HUTCHINSON,[38] one of ELIOT's few surviving friends, was to have seen me. We had a good deal of correspondence about arranging our meeting in London. The night before I was to go up, she telephoned in considerable agitation, and apparently in some indignation as well, and announced that she had just discovered this veto. She said to me, as nearly as I can recollect: "Are we not to respect his wishes?" The only answer I could make to her at the time was: "Well, MRS. HUTCHINSON, under the circumstances – no." But I particularly resented her implication that I was trying to see her under false pretenses, and wrote her at some length to explain that this was not so, and that there was a case for writing ELIOT's life. She did not see me, however.

There was another ELIOT, THOMAS H., the Chancellor of Washington University at St. Louis, which T. S. ELIOT's grandfather had founded, and of which he had also been Chancellor. When I wrote to him and announced my intention of coming to St. Louis, my hopes of seeing him, and the terms of ELIOT's veto, he wrote back and said he didn't consider himself bound by them, as he was only a fifth cousin. So another practical question arose: how close a relation did you have to be to consider yourself a member of the ELIOT family and therefore bound by ELIOT's veto?

In September, my wife and I made a very quick trip to the States. We were there only twelve days, mostly in New York, St. Louis and Boston and I went to New Haven to see Donald Gallup, the bibliographer of ELIOT. He gave me the news that VIVIENNE ELIOT's brother, MAURICE HAIGH-WOOD, was still alive, although he could not give me his address. He said he could be reached through Sotheby's, where he had recently sold some manuscripts. DR. GALLUP also advised me to read as

---

38 Mary Hutchinson.

many letters of ELIOT as I could lay my eyes on, whether or not I could use them in the book, simply to get a flavour of his character. He also advised me to read or search as many of the books, pamphlets and periodicals in his bibliography as I could, as in that way I might dig up some unexpected biographical facts.

In New York I was able to see the famous typescript of The Waste Land, edited and cut by EZRA POUND. The typescript had been given to JOHN QUINN by ELIOT, and had found its way into the New York Public Library, where it was reposing in a special collection. I was only allowed to see it by special permission, and was not allowed to take notes. DR. GALLUP was uniquely privileged to do this, however, and six months or a year before had written an article about it for The Times Library Supplement, in which he reproduced two pages of the typescript. DR. GALLUP told me that the reason this manuscript, scheduled for publication, had been postponed several times, was that MRS. ELIOT, who had a hand in the production, was anxious to make it a perfect piece of scholarship. As a scholar himself, his only comment on this was a small smile.

The three big ammunition dumps of ELIOT material are at the Houghton Library in Harvard, the University Library at Austin, Texas,[39] and at King's College Library in Cambridge, England. On this trip I didn't attempt to see the Library at Texas, but the Librarian, MRS. HIRTH, very kindly sent me a list of the ELIOT material I would be allowed to see if I went there, and we both agreed that the trip would not be worth it.

Much the same thing was true of the Houghton Library at Harvard. I went there but didn't ask to see any ELIOT material. They wouldn't have shown it to me if I had. I did, however, talk to the Curator of Manuscripts, MR. RODNEY DENNIS, who told me that in all his experience of dealing with the widows and daughters of eminent writers who had

---

39 The University of Texas Library.

left bequests of papers, with certain restrictions, he had never come across anything so drastic in its restrictive conditions as this one. He added that he did not think that ELIOT's veto could succeed. He thought that if you suppressed facts here, they have a tendency to pop there.

In Boston I did manage to have tea with two cousins, I think or, at least old friends of ELIOT – the MISSES ROSAMUND and AIMEE LAMB. They invited me for tea in their flat, 301 Berkeley Street. It was a most Bostonian occasion. MISS AIMEE had just returned from a concert in which, she said, the Ravel was good, the Mozart a little too long, and the Piston, on the whole, quite exciting. It was not only Bostonian, it was Eliotesque. We swayed in the wind like a field of ripe corn. Both the ladies at the same time but MISS ROSAMUND provided the obbligato and MISS AIMEE carried the melody. They had obviously not been warned against me, and I couldn't bring myself to warn them. Neither could I bring myself to ask them any questions. When we said goodbye they told me to be sure, when I got back to England, to give their love to dear VALERIE. I smiled and bowed, feeling like a villain.[40]

One day we drove to Gloucester, Massachusetts to see the house built there by ELIOT's father and the present owner, MR. RAYMOND MITNIK, undertook to guide us to the Dry Salvages, but he was not very well acquainted with the countryside and the rocks of which I took pictures turned out to be the wrong ones.

ELAINE BINNEY, an old friend of PAM's,[41] was once engaged to JOHN HAYWARD, cripple who shared a flat with ELIOT for nine years at Cheyne Walk and who died in 1965, the same year

---

40 Rosamund and Aimee Lamb were unmarried sisters and cousins of T. S. Eliot. Rosamund was born in 1898 and Aimee in 1894. After both of them died, their letters from Eliot were donated to the Boston Athenaeum.
41 Pamela Firth Peniakoff was the third of Matthews's three wives; Martha Gelhorn, the third wife of Ernest Hemingway, was his second.

as TSEI had met HAYWARD two or three times, now I found some of his friends very helpful. He and she grew up together in Wimbledon, an address of which he was not proud. The first signs of his disease appeared at eighteen when he was an undergraduate at King's College, Cambridge. Before that he walked, drove a car and so on. For two years, in the thirties, he and her mother and she shared a house in London. He was, perhaps unintentionally, cruel and said anything that came into his head without regard for people's feelings. But he had charm and was very good about putting up with his affliction you couldn't be angry with him when you thought about that. But he was malicious. He never did any original writing. His father and uncle were both doctors. His mother, like JOHN, was outspoken. He had a brother, GEORGE, whom ELAINE liked very much when they were young; he was more attractive than JOHN. Then we went off to Australia, and when he came back he seemed shrunken and dried up, the life gone out of him. JOHN never went to see any of his family, and they never came to see him. After their household (her mother, JOHN and herself) broke up, he got a flat, a ground-floor bed sitting-room, by himself.

When war came, LIONEL (was it LIONEL?) ROTHSCHILD[42] invited him to come and stay in Cambridge, and he did. After the war, he and ELIOT shared a flat at Cheyne Walk. HAYWARD liked to do the talking himself. As he got older he became more so in all particulars. One friend of HAYWARD's, OLIVER LOW, told me about him. This man & H. had met during the war when HAYWARD was living in Cambridge and the other men stationed there in the Army. He got to know HAYWARD quite well and grew very fond of him. Their friendship continued after the war, in London. He told me that one of HAYWARD's great pleasures was to sit in his window and look down at Cheyne Walk, where he could see a bench on which nursemaids or pretty girls occasionally sat, and this gave him great pleasure, especially if they had good legs. According to him,

---

42 It was actually Nathaniel Mayer Victor Rothschild, the 3rd Baron Rothschild.

this gazing at the bench became a great thing in HAYWARD's life and anything that interfered with it was taken quite seriously. Occasionally HAYWARD would ring up his friend in a very dejected frame of mind, and his friend would say: "Bench trouble?" Whereupon HAYWARD would usually say "Yes" and tell him what was the matter. Once, apparently, the bench had been moved by some busybodies so that it was no longer within HAYWARD's view. He summoned his friend and, supervising the operation himself, they managed to get it back in its proper position and anchored it so it couldn't be moved. But once, HAYWARD wanted him to get a ladder and climb up a tree at night to cut off the top, which obstructed his view. He drew the line at that.

My wife and I, though we had failed to see the Dry Salvages, went on a pilgrimage to Burnt Norton, East Coker and Little Gidding. Burnt Norton is a large manor house, the seat of the Earls of Hawtrey[43], which had been burnt in 1737 or earlier, hence the name apparently; and is now a boy's school of fifty maladjusted boys.[44] We arrived there on the first day of term, and asked a master we met in a courtyard if we could have come at a worse time. He agreed that we probably couldn't have. Then he assigned us a couple of boys, one white and one black, to show us around. We saw the formal garden on the side of the hill, the steep sweeping lawns, the large circular pool and fountain, both dry, and another strange V-shaped pool, also dry. From the balustraded terrace there was a sweeping view of the Cotswolds. ELIOT was brought here by EMILY HALE, ~~a girl I know very little about, but who has recently died, and whom I believe at one point hoped to marry ELIOT when he was free~~ who is a story in herself, which I'll mention later.

East Coker, in Somerset, a few miles south of Yeovil, is the place where his family lived for generations, and from which his ancestor emigrated to America. As my wife said, it's

---

43 Actually, the Earls of Harrowby.
44 Burnt Norton was used as a school for boys after World War II.

every American's idea of an English village. Stone cottages with thatched roofs, and gabled caps over doorways; masses of roses, hydrangeas, valerian, dahlias, honeysuckle. The cottage next to the pub has a sign over the door: "Saxon Cellar Discotheque." The church, small and musty-smelling, on the side of the hill above the village, contains an oval stone plaque on the west wall, marking the place where ELIOT's ashes are buried, with these words: "In my beginning is my end. Of your charity, pray for the repose of the soul of THOMAS STEARNS ELIOT, poet. 26th September, 1988 – 4th January, 1965. In my end is my beginning."

And a framed Victorian notice in the porch reads:

Hints to those who worship God in this Church. 1) Be in time. 2) Go straight into church. 3) Kneel down on your knees. 4) Do not look round every time the door opens. 7) Do not whisper to your neighbour.

Little Gidding is in Bedfordshire. Bleak moorland countryside, tiny hamlet, half-deserted farm, and a minute chapel-like church with no congregation. It is served by the Vicar of Great Gidding. He came over to show us the place, and told us there was an annual procession of Friends of Little Gidding in July, led by the Bishop of Ely, as this is in his Diocese. There was once a manor house here, destroyed by the Cromwellians because JOHN FERRAR, the owner, had sheltered the fugitive being Charles 1, overnight.[45]

I found that not every man's hand was against me – or woman's either. The list of those who were helpful to me took up several printed pages in my book. But in general the ELIOT family and close friends, and what I might call the ELIOT Establishment, closed ranks and would have nothing to do with me.

---

[45] John Ferrar was the brother of Nicholas Ferrar, credited for founding the community.

The reason this project has generated so much emotion, it seems to me, is because there is a moral question concerned. What right has anybody to dig into somebody else's life against the wishes of that person? I think most people sympathize with the quatrain in the church at Stratford which is supposed to have been written by SHAKESPEARE:

Good friend, for Jesus' sake forbear
To dig the dust enclosed here.
Bless'd be the man that spares these stones
And curs'd be he that moves my bones.

                (or something like that).
We applaud and sympathize with a man, especially what we call a great man, a prominent man, who wants to keep himself private and keep his private life separate from his public life, on the grounds that it is of no concern to anyone but himself. We sympathize with that; we even applaud it. How then can there be a case for going against ELIOT's expressed wish?

I think MR. NEVIL COGHILL, in a letter to me, has put the case quite squarely, if not altogether fairly. He thinks there are two true and opposite answers:

> For all those who feel they belong to the Eliot family or faction the answer must be: "Leave the skeletons in our cupboard alone; they are ours, not yours," And I sympathize, and I suspect you do too. But for all those who take the side of posterity, and are no respecters of persons (however inquisitive about them they may be), the other answer is true: "Posterity, from whom no secrets should be hid." Tommy Moore burnt Byron's diaries in the grate of John Murray, the publisher (they still show it to you with pride), presumably because they made

no bones about Byron's bisexuality, and this was not to be revealed to the contemporaries of Queen Victoria. If you are on Tommy's side, you are against Posterity. And why not? I have no special regard for it, whereas I can imagine Byron would snort with rage and contempt if every proletarian nose could smell out his sexual extravagances. I should be on his side in this, as I have sympathy with those who put privacy above publicity. On the other hand, if I were a biographer of Byron I would think Tommy a criminal, robbing posterity of a salacious thrill or throb. I can feel the pull (as a critic) of a wish to know everything about a poet in order to 'explain' his poetry. I am a critic myself. But I have always despised my job – we critics are all parasites, and no more necessary than guides in the rambling gardens of artistic creation. However, one has to be what one is, or perhaps one is what one has to be. I try to be a parasite that does not prey upon its host. Fortunately for me, the three poets upon whom I have spent most thought, Chaucer, Langland and Shakespeare, have no biographies, and never will have, at least as far as their privacies are concerned. So I am not tempted to play the psychiatrist critic in their cases.

    Turning to TSE, a great deal, in my opinion more than enough, is in the public domain about him. All his opinions are published, his letters are being prepared for publication, the main and necessary facts are known. An excellent and sufficient biography, even a critical one, is perfectly possible to write now, or will be when the letters are published. No doubt there were unhappinesses is his first marriage. So there are in many a marriage. Is it our business? Is there any problem in any of Eliot's writings that is insoluble unless we know whether

he drive his wife mad, or she him? I don't know of one.
Would The Family Reunion be any less interesting if
it were anonymous? Obviously not. But the spokesman
for Posterity is absolute in his demand for the Whole
Truth. And who knows what that can have been? How can
one find out?

'Well,' Posterity will say, 'ask his friends and
relatives, Bonamy Dobrée, for instance: he's a scholar
who must, or may, have some regard for posterity.' And
if you ask him you are doing right. You are trying
for truth. But if he refuses, he will be right, for he
is preserving privacy; and I hold that at the Day of
Judgment the trial will be conducted in secrecy. Or
God's justice will be cruel.

So, if I may sum up this windy argument, I
hold there is nothing dishonourable in seeking
information from every available source, public
or private. This only means that you value the
wishes of posterity more than those of T. S. Eliot –
a possible position, even for his biographer. On
the other hand, there is nothing dishonouring
or furtive in concealing material and refusing
inquiry if you make the opposite judgment. I
applaud you; I applaud Mrs. Eliot. As a critic, I
feel I already know quite enough about him (in
the public domain) to be able accurately to assess
and appreciate and apprehend his work. He is only
important for his work; he is not important for
having married a wife who went mad.

DR. HUNT (the Curator of Manuscripts at the Bodleian, who
refused to let me see VIVIENNE ELIOT's papers) is certainly
within his rights. There is no law here that obliges owners
of documents, private papers, correspondence, etc., to put
them on public show. Manuscripts are frequently left to
librarians <u>on condition</u> that they are not to be given to

the public for a certain stipulated time. This has no doubt happened in the case of the Eliot Bodley collections. At the same time, there is now law that forbids you to ask for them, not even a moral law as far as I can see.

But are we, is posterity, really only interested in documents that have hitherto been suppressed about a person's life because we are after "a salacious thrill or throb," or is it because human beings have an insatiable (and quite justifiable) curiosity about other human beings (particularly about those exceptional human beings who can express themselves) because only from the life of another human being can we learn about our own lives, about ourselves? The question surely is not whether ELIOT drove his wife mad – or she him – but <u>why</u> she went mad? Apart from the moral question involved (was it wrong to write a life of ELIOT; was it wrong to try to find out facts which he wished concealed?) there were practical difficulties: for example, before I knew that his family, according to VALERIE ELIOT, were also arrayed against me, I had written to the only one I knew well, MRS. THEODORE STURTEVANT, of Newport. (I had known her for twenty-five years or so) and asked her to write me everything that she could remember about her cousin Tom. She did, and then we both discovered (I rather think I told her), about this veto, forbidding "the family" to give any information. She was quite upset, and I was in a quandary about whether or not I was allowed to use the facts, such as they were, that she had given me.

FRANCES LINDLEY seems to think that I can still write a formal biography if I concentrate on ELIOT's early days in America; but I doubt it very much. I am looking forward to seeing the unpublished dissertation at Brown University, which I am to be allowed to read, I believe, and I hope take notes on, or get a photo-copy of. But I think that's already been made what use can be made of it, by HOWARTH, in a book of his, <u>Notes on Some Figures Behind T. S. ELIOT</u>.]

So, the prospects are – what? I don't know. Excelsior.

January 26, 1970 Cyrilly Abels (literary agent) to TSM

Dear Tom: It sounds to me like a dream assignment, Frances has kept me informed, with Xeroxes of her letters, and now I only' hope that Mrs. Eliot will see you. If she sees you, I am sure that she will give her consent.

Actually, I think that not only are you exactly the right person to do this book, but that it's an excellent project, one that most people would not think of doing, one that can be very important, and one which you are eminently suited to doing.

I have met Mrs. Eliot only once, through Bob Giroux, who is an old acquaintance of mine, Bob is very jealous of his relationship with Mrs. Eliot (and before that, with T. S.) but I hope he will see that this book would not interfere with any number of books that others might want to write. Bob is pretty close. An impression stays with me that he joined them on their honeymoon! As I remember, it was in the Bahamas and it really was shortly after their marriage in England.

I shall look forward to good news. With best regards to you and Pam. Sincerely,

February 3, 1970 Frances Lindley to Cyrilly Abels

Dear Cyrilly, Here is Mrs. Eliot's letter. I called England to say that I would meet Tom and Pam in Venice on March 11th, and read Mrs. Eliot's letter to Pam on the phone. She took a rather gloomier view of it than we do here. She mentioned the existence of a substantial collection of Eliot letters in Cambridge some 22 miles from them, but fears that access to them will be prohibited.

You will recall that a year ago Mrs. Eliot wrote us to say that Giroux would be publishing the Eliot

Letters. Can you think. of some way of finding out when they plan to publish and who the editor of the Letters is to be? In a hurry,

June 30, 1970 Barbie Sturtevant to TSM

Dear Jane – Our warmest felicitations! What a great task you have been challenged to undertake! Please forgive delay – actually, the garden and the usual interruptions of too many people forever popping in are <u>not</u> responsible, nor my incurable habit of procrastination – all of the weeks with no answer to your letter have been spent (while gardening etc.) in <u>thinking</u>, an exercise to which I am most unaccustomed!

    First of all may I make two suggestions? It seems to me that it would be worthwhile to write to my brother in Japan, and to plan to see my aunt, Eleanor Hinkley, in Cambridge, when next you are here. My brother, Holmes Welch, is the youngest of my three brothers – twelve years younger than I, and the member of my generation who knew Cousin Tom by far the best <u>intellectually</u>, as "Homie" is himself writing. He is a Sinologist – in Japan at present for an indefinite stay – writing his third book of a trilogy on Buddhism. I believe that Cousin Tom gave Homie considerable assistance with the publishing of his first book on "Taoism" many years ago. Homie saw Cousin T. in London, a very short time before he died, and, of course, whenever Cousin T. was in this country. I will write H. and tell him that you will write to him, probably. His address is: Holmes H. Welch c/o UE, Ichoda-Cho 13, Matsugazaki, SA Kyo-ku, Japan.

    The damnedest address – be sure to <u>print</u>, he says! H. is rather my favorite brother – we "communicate" and share our "problems" despite a vast disparity in brains and years. He is a rather remarkable guy, and I think that Cousin T. thoroughly enjoyed him and was a tiny bit pleased to have that sort of young cousin. Obviously, H. knew Cousin T. in an entirely different way that I did.

 My aunt in Cambridge, without any doubt, knows more of Cousin T. for more years, than anyone alive. He was like her brother during his boyhood and college years. She is now 79 – and remembers the past with amazing clarity. She is a spinster, and my mother's only sister. She has lived in the same house in Cambridge since she was born (in itself a rare feat in these times!!) and it was to this house that Cousin T. came as a boy at Milton Academy and a young man at Harvard – my grandmother was his "family" in Boston when he first came east to school, and his parents were still in St. Louis. My aunt shared a lot with Cousin T. during their youth – she began to write in her "teens" and finally did have her play "Rear Fame" put on in New York, by Eva La Galliano (sp?) the Repertory Theatre. She wrote many plays – all <u>near</u> successes! Again, she was the one of <u>her</u> generation who was closets to Cousin T. <u>intellectually</u> – she has <u>boxes</u> of his letters to her, which she will leave to the Houghton Library at Harvard – they go back to his early college days and are enormously interesting and revealing. I do not know how either my aunt or Valerie would feel about giving you access to them. They would surely be invaluable, however, and it would be worth a try. I am sure you will charm "Yaya" (my aunt) so completely that there will be no problem, only that she would have to check it out with Valerie.

 Much of their correspondence was a discussion of "shop" – but also there are a lot of family problems etc. which would not be of much interest to you. It seems to me that a talk with my beloved "Yaya" would be of the utmost use for you. It is funny – my grandmother was a violent "teetotaller" – when she died at 88, my aunt was totally exhausted, having spent several years taking care of her mother (a very strong willed and dominating woman) – and my mother drove over to Cambridge every day with a large thermos of eggnog (into which she had poured a liberal slug of rum!). My aunt drank it happily and innocently, and it did her worlds of good! Subsequently we got her to drink sherry and now she is an artist with martinis – you don't have to drink gin – she keeps all kinds of booze on hand!

Please forgive such time consuming digressions! As for me – well – my memories of Cousin T. are, I fear, of little or no use to you! To answer your questions, however, here goes! I saw him most at my aunt's house in Cambridge, where there was a family cocktail party – just my brothers, their wives and my sons and theirs – every time he came for the last ten years before his death – and, lunching alone with him and Valerie at the Continental Hotel in Cambridge – before he varied V. usually in Cambridge or at my mother's in Milton. Cape Anne was long before I was born. My mother had the most important snapshots of her girlhood reprinted just before she died in 1958, and made a special book – it is very interesting – picture of Cousin T. in a 'sou'wester cruising with Ma and Pa – all the Eliots at Cape Anne, Cousin T. as a young man in Cambridge, etc. The book is a real treasure of me, and I think it would give anyone writing a biography of T. S. Eliot a sort of feeling and atmosphere. It is in our living room, and when you come you can look it over. I truly believe that your greats source is "Yaya," however. She is most amusing, and bright, and not <u>at all</u> spinsterish <u>conversationally</u>, or in her thinking.

Now (and I'll try to condense my thoughts), what troubles me most about writing to you about Cousin T. is that it seems almost impossible to express my <u>feelings</u> clearly. I feel a responsibility to explain <u>why</u> I adored him as I did, and as I am basically a very reserved person I have a horror of writing like Queen Victoria (whom I really do think was a <u>great</u> person, however).

The first time that I ever <u>remember</u> seeing Cousin T. was in London in 1922. My parents had taken my brother and me abroad for the first time. I was twelve, so clearly my reactions are valueless, and unreliable. We went for tea with Cousin T. and Vivien. I had just been reading a gorgeously illustrated edition of "The Idylls of the King," where "Viven" was a gorgeous, auburn haired, romantically dressed beauty, and expected that this new cousin I was about to meet must have a wife who looked like the Tennyson's Vivien. To my great confusion Cousin T.'s wife was very thin, pale and her face was surrounded by masses of soft, black clouds of hair. She was silent and fragile, and totally unaware of <u>us</u>! She rather repelled and frightened me – she was <u>strange</u>! They had a dear cat, and I loved cats, as did Cousin T. always. I can't separate what I saw and felt from what I may have overheard my parents saying later. There seemed to be all sorts of problems and worries about Vivien and something about Cousin T. and Pa – all of these vague memories of a twelve year old are valueless – just "gossipy" inaccuracies. The only clear and true memory is that I <u>did</u> feel something mysterious and strange in Vivien and that Cousin T. was <u>trying very hard</u> in some way – and that he liked <u>me</u>!

After that I saw him whenever he came here and whenever I was in England which was almost every year. There are no special memories – I was at the age to be very involved with myself, and remember mostly the young men I dashed around with, though now I can't even remember most of them!

During my married years in Boston I was fairly occupied with four small children, and saw Cousin T. only in a vague sort of way. He did write that verse about bears for my oldest son on his first Xmas for my grandmother to put in a baby book for her first great grandchild. It hangs beside our fireplace. (I must have it xeroxed.)

When my three sons and I went abroad in 1953, Ebby was a junior at Harvard and the twins sophomores. Almost the high point of our glorious successful, totally memorable three months of going and seeing and doing all that I did in my youth with my parents was seeing Cousin T. in London. My son, Ben (who is married to Alexandra C.) was in a slat of anticipatory delirious. Cousin T. came for cocktails with us at our hotel, the Basil Street, where apparently Cousin T. usually put up his nieces etc. I have an amusing little note from him doubting the ability of the Basil Street to make a decent martini. He was so dear with my boys – none of us will ever forget it. Ben told him that he had also lived in his room at Milton Academy and they had a splendid discussion of Milton "then and now." Cousin T. was still smoking in those days, even though he'd been told to give it up, and how he did enjoy his gin and cigarettes! He was very funny – we all laughed a lot. He had such an original collection of adjectives when describing people, which made us laugh. It was such a success – the dear man, he perfectly knew what it meant to these three young men, (because they all had read everything he ever wrote) to spend a cozy hour with him. He made it perfect, and I am <u>sure</u> he enjoyed it! As for me, excepting for his plays, his genius is lost on me. My appreciation of poetry has stopped with Tennyson and Kipling. Unless it rhymes and has rhythm it means nothing to me – honesty is the best policy, and so I never discussed anything of that sort with Cousin T. or even mentioned his writing. Our friendship was entirely "family" and non-intellectual. I'm sure he perfectly understood, with his acute perceptiveness, that I was a totally unintellectual person and not bright at all, and he didn't mind – I think, not like all great people – he liked different people for a variety of reasons. He certainly enjoyed attractive females and alluring clothes and glamorous hats and liked to be treated as an <u>attractive man</u>, not first as a great poet, an awe inspiring literary figure. He certainly <u>was</u> an attractive man!!! Even the last time I saw him, though he was not at all well, he still had that quality of male charm, which for me, always overshadowed his imposing personality as a "great," so that I thought of him without of any of that.

    However, when I think of him, first of all I am moved by the remembrance of his <u>kindness</u>! He was a rarely sensitive and unselfish man, and he therefore understood and had true sympathy. The best example of this was the last time I had lunch with him and Valerie in the hotel in Cambridge. I had just lost my second grandson in a little over a year. My first grandchild had died in England (where Ebby was studying at Cambridge) at the age of 5 months – very suddenly, what they call a "crib death." His mother found him dead when she went to pick him up to feed him – he had been perfectly well an hour before – no explanation.

A year later my son Roger had a son, and named him after Ted – we were enormously touched and proud that they would name a child after Roger's stepfather. They came east for Christmas and little Teddy died in exactly the same way in Boston on their way to us for Christmas. It was a dreadful blow for all of us and I was truly shattered – especially as it was the <u>second</u> time, for another son – one wondered what curse there was in the family? All silly, just bad luck, but it was very hard.

Cousin T. and Valerie were in Cambridge. I had been unable to go to the family party for them, because it was the day of the service for Teddy, and Roger and Sue were coming here. However, Valerie called and begged me to lunch with them the next day, as they were leaving soon. I didn't <u>feel</u> like it a bit – I was completely tired out with trying to help R. & L. and be both cherry and comforting, and my heart ached too much to make any more effort over anyone. However, I went up to Cambridge, and how glad I have been ever since! Those two dear people helped me so much! Although Cousin T. had never had children, he <u>knew</u> exactly how it was. We talked a little about Roger and Lee, and about the baby – both of them made me <u>able</u> to <u>talk</u> – because I felt they <u>felt</u>! And then the conversation drifted away to other areas, and we had such a dozy, warm and satisfying talk. I left them feeling strengthened and optimistic. Valerie is a <u>dear</u> girl – she has a warm heart, and she is so direct and unartificial! They loved each other, I think, as <u>much</u> or more than anyone I've ever known. Perhaps it was their feeling for each other and dependence on one another that gave them such a capacity to comfort me.

Now – there it is. You poor man! My writing is ghastly, my total incapacity to condense appalling – my punctuation confusing, and my thinking muddled. This <u>all</u> I can think of – I'm sure the facts are not of any use, such as they are. How can one describe Cousin Tom? He was so <u>gentle</u> – perhaps that above all – his modesty and gentleness and humour – his quiet and relaxed way of sitting down to a "give and take" chat. He <u>never</u> pontificated – he <u>listened</u>. He was a delightful man and a very lovable one to spend the "cocktail hour" with. Being with him <u>did one good</u>! What more can I add?

    Little help as I've been, you will, surely, get something of value from my brother and my aunt.

    Now may I <u>strongly</u> recommend that when you come here you stay in our guest house? You have total privacy and independence there – the kitchen is <u>most</u> thoroughly equipped and the living room <u>comfortable</u> and rather attractive and the bedrooms, bathroom are adequate. You can have your own schedule, go out, and entertain when and whom you like, and if I may say so be a lot more comfortable than in any of the houses of your kind friends. As <u>we</u> are famously impossible guests, because we cannot endure the lack of independence of visiting, and the lack of privacy, we pity the miseries you are forced to endure whenever you visit "our island."

    Do consider making a brave break with tradition and this time tell your devoted friends that you are staying in the Little Cave, but will be happy to lunch or dine with them. We truly recommend it – and from here I can drive you to Cambridge to see "Yaya" without the schedule affecting anyone. It may be a rather long day! Needless to say we should be thrilled to have you here – we promise not to cross the driveway unless invited – you have a telephone there – in fact, it pretty well has everything, including most efficient electric heat. After Labour

Day it will be unoccupied for the winter, excepting for my sons on an occasional weekend.

Ted is fine! Has fifty pots set – has splendid help, and is learning, as I am to pace himself. We do not stay out late, when we have a "big" evening he rests the next morning – above all we are learning not to "fight the clock" – that is the whole secret, and the hardest of all to learn, as I, in particular, have spent my first sixty years "running." Ted looks marvelouly, and feels well. He is scared enough, thank heaven, to obey doctor's orders, and we feel that as long as we don't relax the rule, we should be avoiding any more problems. The ghastly fright of last October is still clear in my memory – I <u>still</u> wake each a.m. feeling thankful that the night is over and all is well – Ted too. Perhaps this will pass with time – I hope so!

Thank you, thank you, for the <u>exquisite</u> photography of you and Pam – bless you for sending them to us! They <u>made</u> our <u>Christmas</u>! And have been enjoyed by all your friends. <u>What</u> fun it must have been to see them when they came out of that machine – Ted and I did this once at the Providence station – in black and white – and the results of staggering – a joy forever after. He looked like a gangster and I like hell! You were such dears to share them with us, and I'm so ashamed that I never thanked you – nor, for your incredible memory in sending the Talkin??'s address. You are <u>the only</u> person I knew who actually <u>does do</u> what they promise – a quality which I admire more than any other, as I am so hopeless. We are very indebted to you – and very ashamed of all the months of silence and – well – I am sorry, and T. is ashamed of me! But, I <u>mildly</u> inquire at times, <u>he</u> can write sometimes, but he says that is "woman's work." It is truly exciting that you are to be "the one" – but I must say that Harper & row could not have made a wiser decision and they are very fortunate that you are willing to plunge into such a vast project – fascinating, challenging, and a hell of a lot of hard, hard work. Nobody else could do it as well and you will, I'm sure, find that once you get into it, it will carry you along – Cousin Tom will!!!

With lots and lots of love to you and Pam from both of us and eager anticipations of your moving into the "Little Cave" for a long visit – Penitently, Barbie.

[Added at top of page 1] "Yaya" has been asked by the BBC to do some sort of a TV interview about Cousin Tom, because after talking to the ELIOTs they felt she had much more to offer! This will be next fall.

July 16, [1970]

I met FRANK MORLEY for lunch at the Garrick. I had met him once or twice before with mutual friends and put him down as a <u>faux bonhomme</u>. Our meeting today made me think also that he was pretty cagey. We had a little in common, but not much. We're both Americans, had both been to New College, Oxford, and were both members of the Garrick. He had been allegedly a close friend of ELIOT's, and a colleague on the board of Faber & Faber. In a letter written to me after out meeting, he said: "Such advice or information as I have already given, or could give, in entirely sub rosa. If, so to speak, I was being interviewed, you would agree, I think, I ought to see, and approve, any transcript. Whatever I have already written about ELIOT is, of course, in the public domain. I mentioned the possibility that I might be doing some writing myself about the twenties and thirties; if so, ELIOT would come into it, and that's another matter which might have some bearing. I sympathise with your problem; you must also sympathise with mine."

The one interesting piece of information he did give me, perhaps inadvertently, was to say that ELIOT's feeling about his first marriage was one of more than remorse, it was one of guilt, and what looked like exaggerated guilt. I gathered, although perhaps this is taking Morley's hints too far, that ELIOT seemed to have felt that he had betrayed the secrets of their marriage in his poetry.

November 24, [1970]

I went to Oxford to see NEVILE COGHILL, Emeritus Fellow of Merton. COGHILL met at the gate at Merton and we talked in a private room over a glass of sherry for about an hour or so. He hadn't heard about the veto and seemed somewhat taken aback when I tried to state my case and he seemed to feel a kind of benevolent neutrality about the whole affair. When I told him another one of the purposes I had come to Oxford today was to go to the Bodleian, or to ask his advice about whether I should go to the Bodleian, to try to see VIVIENNE ELIOT's papers there, he said he would come with me to make sure that I was made a reader of the Library. This turned out to be unnecessary; all I had to do was announce myself a senior member of the University, which they would check up on, and then ask to see the papers I wanted.

I had got my researcher, PAT GARRATT, to get me a copy of VIVIENNE ELIOT's will from Somerset House, and in that will I found a most interesting paragraph, Number 5:

> I give to the Bodleian Library, Oxford, absolutely and free of duty, all my papers, manuscripts, diaries, journals, photographic albums and sketches, except securities and books of account, on condition that the said Library shall not permit any of the same to be altered, erased, added to, quoted from, or used for the purposes of any work of fiction.

The librarian to whom I made my first application said that he remembered such a collection, but would have to consult his colleague. When I first tried to get across to VIVIEN's papers in the Bodleian, COGHILL left for a lunch engagement, and I waited to see MR. HUNT, who I believe, is the Curator of Manuscripts in the Bodleian. When he appeared, he said he remembered the collection very well; he had been through it when it was first acquired in 1948 – the year after VIVIENNE's death – and no one, he said, was to be allowed to see it until everyone concerned was dead. ROBERT SENCOURT[46] (who now fulfils the condition of being dead) who had nearly finished a biography of ELIOT, had apparently got wind of this bequest, and had been turned away. MR. HUNT said that very few people, so far, knew of it but if there was any sort of hue and cry he would probably put the collection under the protection of VALERIE ELIOT. I asked him by what legal right the Bodleian could behave this way, and he said, quite serenely, that libraries made their own rules in these cases, and that they were well within their rights.

November 30, [1970]

I went to London and took a train to Lewes, to see PHILIP MAIRET, former Editor of The New English Weekly, who had succeeded ORAGE[47], and was also a great friend of ELIOT's. MR. MAIRET was 84, a small, deaf, frail figure, who seemed at

---

46 On August 25, 1931 TSE wrote to Emily Hale: "Did I ever answer your enquiry about the man you met with us? His name is Robert Esmonde Gordon George — a New Zealander — ex-officer in the Bengal Lancers — sent up to Oxford late, after the war — Roman Catholic convert, and very devout — always buzzing about with Cardinals and Abbots — lives in Hyeres, having poor health — and seems to know an immense number of people everywhere — writes under the name of Robert Sencourt — I believe his recent Life of the Empress Eugenie was very successful both here and in America. He is inclined to take a little too much upon himself, but otherwise is a very refined and sensitive person, and I like his company. Very eager interest in human beings."

47 Alfred Richard Orage founded the publication in 1932.

first donnish-pedantic, and innocent; then showed flashes of something steelier. He told me, as soon as he let me in, that if he had been able to forestall me he would have, as he was supposed to go to a funeral that day. He knew about the veto, seemed non-committal about it, although he did say that he thought VALERIE ELIOT was in an ambiguous position. He thinks that what she should probably do, and probably will do eventually, is to appoint an official biographer – "English, of course." Naturally, he had never heard of me, or anything I had written, and seemed non-committal about me too. But he did seem to take it for granted that I was not the right person to write ELIOT's life. I said to him at one point: "Do you think if I were the right man to write about ELIOT that I would know it?" And he, without the slightest hesitation, said: "Yes!" MAIRET knew SENCOURT and had read the nearly finished book that SENCOURT wrote, had found it "pretentious" and urged SENCOURT not to publish it.

December 15, 1970

Went to London and had lunch at Buck's with DAVID GARNETT,[48] age 79, and not very spry. He said that he was recovering from a cold, and coughed a great deal. He is living on a houseboat in the Thames, called <u>Moby Dick</u>, which is afloat at high tide and on the mud at low. Not much heat, I gather, but he says there's enough. He obviously didn't know ELIOT very well, or like him very much; but he did tell an anecdote. One concerned a cocktail party that JONATHAN CAPE[49] gave in London for ROBERT FROST. FROST showed up wearing very hairy tweeds; hair coming out of his ears, hair coming out his nose; "looking like last year's potato," says GARNETT. ELIOT was there; with patent leather hair, patent leather

---

48 David Garnett (1892–1981) was a British novelist and a member of the Bloomsbury Group.
49 Herbert Jonathan Cape founded his eponymous publishing firm in 1921 and managed it until his death in 1960.

clothes, white tie and tails (he was going on to some other
function), with the Order of Merit on a ribbon round his neck:
and GARNETT wished very much that MAX BEERBOHM[50] might have
been on hand to make a cartoon on the American poet who came
abroad, and the American poet who stayed at home.

The other story he told me was about seeing ELIOT at
FRANK MORLEY's[51] farm, which must have been in 1932 (I think
ELIOT stayed there we he came back from America), and
according to GARNETT, Morley and ELIOT told dirty stories.
The example he gave me, which, he said, made ELIOT laugh for
about ten minutes, was about something MORLEY told him about
friends of his who could let farts, and light them – like
human Bunsen burners. ELIOT thought this was very amusing,
and laughed for ten minutes.

GARNETT liked FRANK MORLEY; called him an intellectual
extrovert. He liked him better than ELIOT.

December 17, [1970]

A letter from WILLIAM FRANKEL, commenting on the draft I
had sent to him, at his suggestion; a letter to the Librarian
at the Bodleian (which I think I made a record of). WILLIAM's
reply was not very satisfactory. He thought the draft letter
admirable, but pointed out that if I wrote to him direct,
and he took an adverse position, and committed himself in
writing, it was going to make it very difficult for him to
budge. He suggested that I should get hold of JOHN SPARROW,
the WARDEN of All Souls', who, as I told him, was anti-ELIOT,
and I didn't think I wanted him on my side. But he says:

> ...Couldn't you ask him in the first place whether
> you should send the letter to the Librarian, or

---

50   Sir Henry Maximillian Beerbohm (1872–1956) was an English essayist and caricaturist.
51   Frank Morley (1899–1980) was a friend and colleague of Eliot's at Faber and Faber.

whether he has any better idea on procedure? I can imagine that, in principle, he is the sort of chap who could be relied upon to take up the cudgels on an issue like this,

I don't like the idea. I think I'll ask JAMES FAWCETT, who is a Fellow of All Souls', what he thinks of it.

1971

~~December 31~~ January 1, 1971

Went to London. Saw COLIN OLIVER, my solicitor, in his office, and asked his opinion about whether I had any legal recourse in the matter of the Bodleian Library. He was sympathetic, I think, but not very hopeful; and seemed to agree that 'clout' was the thing that was required.

I think my next step is to write to BILL DEAKIN, and get his opinion on it, and see who he thinks might be on my side, and have the requisite clout. Aside from him, the only people I can think of are RICHARD CROSSMAN, ISAIAH BERLIN, A. J. R. TAYLOR, SIR WILLIAM HAYTER, MAURICE BOWRA, FREDDIE AYER, and DAVID CECIL.

Lunch at Buck's with CYRILLY ABELS, my New York agent, and her husband, JEROME; and told her all about it.

I telephoned to ALAN MACLEAN at Macmillans, to ask him about the SENCOURT book, and he said he was quite sure they were not publishing it (I suppose it must be Macmillans of New York); and I made a date to have lunch with him.

As I told COLIN, whatever happens about this book—whether I get the book done or not—this project will have been worth it as far as I'm concerned. Only yesterday, reading in ARTHUR SYMONDS' The Symbolist Movement, I came on this passage, which settled in my mind about SHAKESPEARE that has always fascinated me:

"There are certain natures, great or small, SHAKESPEARE or RIMBAUD, it makes no difference, to whom the work is nothing; the act of working, everything."

That explains, as far as I'm concerned, why SHAKESPEARE apparently didn't give a damn about seeing his plays published.

Thanks to an introduction from LAURIE LEE, I'm now going to be able to converse with the Poet Laureate, C. DAY LEWIS. It's not as Poet Laureate I want to see him, however, but as the author of an obit on ELIOT for The Times, which he wrote when ELIOT was still alive, based on information which he got from JOHN HAYWARD, I believe, and in which he mentions, very tactfully, the long tragedy of his first marriage. It's about that I want to talk to him. He writes me that I'm to ring him up on Sunday to make a date. I suggested that we might meet at the Athenaeum because he's listed as a member; but he says: "By all means let us have lunch together, preferably not at the Athenaeum, from which I have just resigned in protest against the food!" (This entry should have been headed January 1, 1971, the first of the New Year.)

January 3, [1971]

I've just talked to the Poet Laureate, CECIL DAY LEWIS, on the telephone, and made an appointment to have lunch with him at the Garrick, on Tuesday, the 15th. He tells me that a General Strike, he hears, has been scheduled for that day, but if it doesn't come off, he'll see me there.

January 8, [1971]

At King's College Library today, MUNBY said to me that his friend, JOHN CARTER (I think that's his name; anyway, he was a great friend of HAYWARD's and of MUNBY's, and I think he was the one who got out the pamphlet of memorials on HAYWARD) - MUNBY said that CARTER was going to write a gentle letter to The Listener, wondering why they had said nothing whatever in that BBC programme, about ELIOT's criticism, and there was not a mention of JOHN HAYWARD; and MUNBY said, looking meaningly at me: "I think we know why there was no mention of HAYWARD." I said: "You mean—yes —VALERIE ELIOT." Another wrinkle, and another sub-plot.

January 9, [1971]

This will be in the nature of a digression. A few remarks on a book, or parts of a book, that I've just read, by Henry Sherek, called Not in Front of the Children. Two chapters in this book are alleged to be about ELIOT, and he is mentioned in them a few times. Sherek, the gargantuously gross impresario, was the producer of The Cocktail Party at Edinburgh, London, and in New York, I think; and also The Confidential Clerk; I don't know whether he was in on The Elder Statesman or not. He was a horrible looking man who couldn't have been as horrible as he looked. I met him once and he seems to have remembered the occasion, though very inaccurately. I also saw him twice after that, in Morocco, where I believe he retired; but he obviously didn't remember me, not seeing me in what he thought was my natural habitat.

I found one nice anecdote. After the first night of The Confidential Clerk at the Edinburgh Festival, Sherek and ELIOT were together in the Caledonian Hotel, in Sherek's room, opening telegrams. I'll give it to you in Sherek's words:

> ...at the time did add a new dimension to that extraordinary work. Cosmic despair remained, but private tragedy explained much of its hitherto inexplicable imagery. The dry, parsonical voice

of the poet read his own verse; modern actors interpreted scenes from the plays; by the end we saw Old Possum plain.

Oh, did you!

January 12, [1971]

To London, to have lunch with C. DAY LEWIS, the Poet Laureate, at the Garrick. LEWIS couldn't or wouldn't, tell me anything about ELIOT. I gathered that he didn't like him much; he'd once has a row with him when DAY LEWIS refused to sign a letter sent to him by ELIOT, to the United States Supreme Court, urging them to set aside the sentence on Ezra Pound. LEWIS refused to sign it on the ground that it would be impertinent to interfere in the domestic arrangements of another nation, and expressed himself thus to ELIOT, who wrote him a hot note, misunderstanding his use of the word 'impertinent', which Day Lewis said he meant in the legal sense; and the coolness thus precipitated never altogether warmed up.

    I had wanted to ask him about the <u>TIMES</u> obit of ELIOT, which I was told that he had written with the help of JOHN HAYWARD. DAY LEWIS says that he never read this obit after it appeared, he was abroad at the time; and doesn't feel responsible for any of the facts, which were all given to him by HAYWARD.

    I liked him better than I thought I would. Physically a big man, taller than me, and quite pleasant. When we parted he wished me success. DAY LEWIS knew SENCOURT, and said was, or had been, an Oxford don. He had read SENCOURT's book on ELIOT, and refused to published it. He said it was very bad; and mostly about SENCOURT, not about ELIOT. DAY LEWIS had heard of VIVIENNE, but knew very little about her. He didn't know of BERTRAND RUSSELL's intimacy with the ELIOTs in their early married days, or her contributions to The Criterion, and so forth. When I told him about the thirty lines of heroic couplets written by her, that appeared in the first draft of The Waste Land, his eyebrows went up.

I saw at the Garrick three other members of the literary establishment, JOHN SUTRO, HAROLD ACTON, and STEPHEN SPENDER, but they didn't see me.

March 21, [1971]

The post office strike, recently over, has slowed down a great many different things. VALERIE ELIOT was to have given a BBC talk on The Waste Land on February 28; she has now postponed that until summer, or next autumn, to coincide with the publication of the manuscript of The Waste Land, which has also had its publication postponed. The ROBERT SENCOURT biography of ELIOT which was due to come out in February, after being postponed, has now been postponed again until March, and as March is nearly over, I imagine it has suffered a further postponement.

On January 5, just before the post office strike shut down, I wrote to my friend F. W. DEAKIN, the ex-WARDEN of St. Anthony's College, Oxford, to ask him if he could help me. At the risk of repetition, I'll repeat the letter I wrote to him:

> Dear Bill: Since we are apparently not to meet again on this earth, I am reduced to the expediency of writing you a letter. I'd much rather talk to you for an hour.
>
> In my ripe old age (I'll be 70 in a couple of weeks; can you beat it?) Harper & Row, of New York, have twisted my arm sufficiently to get me to sign a contract for a book on T. S. Eliot. I have three years (from last June) to do it in. Since signing up, I've had ten other offers from publishers, English and American—so you can see there's some interest in the book.

March 26, [1971]

MR. Davin's answer has arrived:

> 22 March, 1971, The Clarendon Press, ? Street, Oxford. Dear Mr. Matthews: Many thanks for your letter of 18 March. I am not sure that I can be very helpful to your with your problem. Since Eliot declared that he did not want a biography of himself to be written, I suppose that Mrs. Eliot is within her rights to ensure that his wishes are carried out. Presumably, also, Mrs. Eliot owns the copyright of the papers that are in Bodley and I guess that they were put there on the condition that she would have the right of veto over whoever might want to see them.
> Again, I believe that an edition of Eliot's letters is being prepared and I know that a Delegate of this Press, Dame Helen Gardner, is in some way involved—she is a personal friend of Mrs. Eliot's
> So you can see that the position is fraught with perils for me also. If nonetheless, you would like to discuss your problem with me I could see you here or in London. I come to London from time to time but should not be likely to be free for about a fortnight yet. If you were coming here, it would probably be easier, provided that I had a few days' notice. Yours sincerely, (an indistinguishable signature).

I don't know why he should presume that the copyrights of the papers that are in the Bodleian are owned by MRS. ELIOT; I take it they are not. And why am I reminded of Coolidge's famous <u>reductio ad absurdum</u> of the problem of the European war debts: "They hired the money, didn't they?"

I'm getting quite a lot of good advice these days. This is from a letter from my brother-in-law, Spack: "What you should do with the peripheries of the ELIOT research is to imitate the French and do a separate (and sardonic) book on the research itself. It ought to be quite funny (which is a talent you have anyhow, God knows)—an en marge de, in short."

And this from my son, PAUL: "Did I ever tell you my idea, or suggestion, about you and the ELIOT book? No? It's this: that all the biographies that are being done now, or recently, are huge factual tomes which the biographer himself stays out of completely, offering no opinions, giving no slants, presenting no cases or arguments. Strikes me that you could make a critical killing (particularly since you are scarce on facts) by coming on heavy with the opinions, insights, arguments, special slants, this that and the other, whatever it may be. Your own ideas about ELIOT, in short; backed up, of course, by your research. Because this is the one thing the critics have been complaining about recently, in reviews of big biographies that I have read: that they are lifeless, that the biographers have no strong opinions about their subject, that they lack a point of view. What's that Frost said about a poem being mounted on a prejudice? Of knowing no poem that wasn't?"

March 27, [1971]

After coming to a slow burn and writing an answer that PAM said would simply antagonize him, I finally managed to send MR. DAVIN this reply:

> Dear Mr. Davin: Thank you for your letter of March 22. The papers in Bodley that I want to see are not, to the best of my knowledge and belief, copyright by MRS. ELIOT or under her control—that is the whole point! Her writ is thought to run so far and

wide that she can sequester papers over which she has no legal control. Or can she? I intend to find out.

I do not believe that Mrs. Eliot is within her rights in trying to ensure that no biography of her husband is written. And I believe that until the very end of his life Mr. Eliot was on my side of the argument. Do you know this passage (from a lecture he gave at the University of Minnesota, printed later in <u>The Frontiers of Criticism</u>, 1956)?: 'I do not suggest that the personality and the private life of a dead poet constitute sacred ground on which the psychologist must to tread. The scientist must be at liberty to study such material as his curiosity leads him to investigate—so long as the victim is dead and the laws of libel cannot be invoked to stop him. Nor is there any reason why the biographies of poets should not be written. They are very useful. Any critic seriously concerned with a man's work should be expected to know something about the man's life.'

It seems to me ridiculous to assert and try to ensure that the biography of a man of T. S. Eliot's stature should not be written—and I think that the veto will prove impossible to enforce.

I certainly wouldn't blame you for being cautious and even sceptical about someone you have never seen. Nevertheless, if you are sufficiently interested to hear more, I hope you will suggest a date, either in London or at Oxford, when we can meet. Yours sincerely,

But I haven't much hope getting anything out of this man whom my tough and resourceful friend Bill Deakin described as "tough and resourceful."

March 31, [1971]

Today, MR. DAVIN's reply:

> Dear Mr. Matthews: Man thanks for your letter of 27 March. I am afraid I feel rather out of my depth in this Eliot business. I have no great locus standi and I suppose that Eliot is a Faber's dish rather than ours. I do not want to be unhelpful and I would be glad to listen to your side of the case if that is what you would like to happen. Unfortunately, I am now going off on holiday and will not be back until after Easter. I guess that when I do get back there will be a great pile of work awaiting me, but I am to be in London on 15 April and could offer you lunch at the Traveller's Club if that would suit you. Yours sincerely, D. M. Davin.

I think I am about ready to kiss MR. DAVIN goodbye before I have even said hello to him.

Also this letter from M. MICHEL FABRE, professor at the Sorbonne. I don't know whether I recorded the fact that wrote to his wife, first of all, whom I knew, and asked her if she would like to do some research for me, and when she said she was too busy, she suggester her husband, so I wrote to him. I asked him to find out what he could about T. S. ELIOT in Paris during 1911 and 1912 when he was at the Sorbonne, and particularly about a man named JEAN VERDENAL, to whom his first book was dedicated. This was his letter:

> Dear M. Matthews: I checked at the Sorbonne a first time (teaching there I thought I'd have access to archives which are not normally open to the public) but the results were very disappointing,

> because most of the archives (records, etc.) for the
> first half century are either in some dark place
> in the basements are practically inaccessible, or
> destroyed. But I know a nice secretary who will try
> to help me.
>   As to Verdenal, I managed to contact his niece,
> but she told me that you had already contacted her
> father, M. Verdenal, who lives at Pau (38 Avenue
> Thiers, 64 Pau) or was it somebody else? Then she
> knows even less than her father, of course.
>   I shall keep my eyes open for information
> about Eliot in Paris in 1911/12, but so far, I
> have found nothing. All our best to both of you.
> Michel Fabre.

April 1, [1971]

Rather than pursue this faint-hearted Odysseus any further, I am thinking of seeking the advice of my friend, James Fawcett, who is an international lawyer, a Fellow, or an ex-Fellow of All Souls', and at present has some executive position with Chatham House; to ask him for his advice, and what he would think about enlisting the aid of his WARDEN, JOHN SPARROW.

April 2, [1971]

My reply to the dastardly MR. DAVIN:

> Thank-you for your letter of March 30, and for your
> invitation to lunch at the Travellers' on April 15. I
> had not planned to be in London that day, or I should
> have been happy to accept. I do, however, expect to be
> in Oxford, for a Friends of the Ashmolean expedition,
> on April 27, which is supposed to return about 5 p.m.
> Could you have a drink at the Randolph with my wife

and me about 5.30 or 6.00 that day? We'll be catching
a train to London, but I think there's one about 7.30.
Yours sincerely,

I then rang up my friend, JAMES FAWCETT, at Chatham House,
and made a date to have a drink with him at the Athenaeum
next Tuesday at 6 p.m.

April 5, [1971]

A letter from FRANCES LINDLEY, in New York:

> I am so glad you've turned up someone who seems
> likely to put the heat on that Bodleian bastard.
> No rumour of Eliotic intrigues reaches me, but
> I wonder if it might not be worth the time if you
> were to drop a letter to Donald Gallup and ask him
> how's tricks? From your report of your autumn chat
> with him, he struck me as being pretty au courant
> in respect to the moves and counter-moves,
> and he might have noted some alteration in the
> atmosphere.

To which I replied:

> I'm still treading with the delicacy of Agag in
> the Bodleian matter. The 'tough resourceful' New
> Zealander at the Clarendon Press turns out to be a
> poltroon and a dastard; I haven't completely signed
> him off yet but I'm having a drink tomorrow in London
> with a friend who's an All Souls' Fellow, to see where
> that line leads.

DONALD GALLUP and I correspond (in this game he's
everybody's aunt); here's an excerpt from our latest exchange
(March 16, 26):

>...I can hardly describe the progress of my Eliot research as <u>satisfactory</u>—it can't be altogether <u>that</u> as long as the unbudgeable Valerie stands like Apollyon in the path—but it progresses. And I hope I can continue to count on your patience and forbearance, and perhaps even your sympathy. (I also sent him a published interview of mine with TSE.)

(His answer):

> Thank you very much for...the clipping of your Eliot interview from <u>Mademoiselle</u>. Had I known of this in time, I should certainly have included it in the bibliography. I am grateful to have it now and shall put it into my already bulky file of additions and corrections.
>   Certainly you have my sympathy—as does Valerie, whose position is a difficult if not impossible on. I look forward to the publication of <u>The Waste Land</u> facsimile, which is, I understand, now definite for September.

VALERIE, by the way, has never acknowledged my last letter to her (Dec. 12, 1970) in which I rather disingenuously fished for at least some sort of formal answer, by pointing out three typographical errors in TSE's last published book, <u>To Criticise the Critic</u>.

April 8, [1971]

Day before yesterday I met my friend, JAMES FAWCETT, at the Athenaeum for a drink, and I told him the story about the Bodleian. He said he would see what he could do about getting a friend of his to find out the proper procedure for getting those papers.

This morning I had two letters; one from MR. DAVIN's secretary, saying that he was away at present, but would be in touch with me on his return next week; and the other from JAMES FAWCETT:

> I have spoken to John Bell; he knows about the Eliot papers in the Bodleian, and of your interest in them, and says that it is a 'very delicate' situation. In particular, he says: (1) A biography of Eliot is being written for Faber & Faber. They would not want to see the Bodleian papers in the hands of a competing biographer. Helen Gardner, though not the author of the biography, is involved here; (2) The second wife is editing Eliot's letters and would try to stop any disclosure of the Bodleian papers to anyone else.
>   He thinks that there are only two possible courses: (a) An approach to Fabers to get an agreed common use of the Bodleian papers; or (b) A direct letter to Robert Shackleton, Bodley's Librarian, asking for access to the papers, given the terms of the bequest. He doubts whether (a) would work. I know Charles Monteith well, a director of Fabers, and he might be approached if you think it worthwhile.
>   I am sorry to have achieved so little.
>   We look forward very much to seeing you again.
> Yours ever,

Well, the plot thickens.

I replied:

> Dear James: Thank you for your letter of April 7, for the promptness of your reply, and for your efforts on my behalf.

The news that a biography of Eliot is being written for Faber & Faber is not altogether unexpected—it puts me in mind of the famous tombstone inscribed: 'I expected this, but not so soon.'—but a bin of a blow just the same. I'd like very much to know who the biographer is, and when they expect to publish it. Do you suppose you could find out from your friend Charles Monteith—or is that too much to ask? (and I wonder how they square this with Eliot's veto from the tomb!)

Judging by past experience, I don't think any director of Fabers would so much as give me the time of day; so I'll not ask you at this point to put me in touch with Monteith. Before I do anything further, I think I shall take counsel with myself and perhaps also with my publisher.

Thank you again, etc.

April 8, [1971]

A letter written but not sent, to F. V. MORLEY, Esq.

Dear Frank Morley: Will you give me a straight answer to a straight question?

Has a biography of T. S. Eliot now been authorized by Faber & Faber and Mrs. Eliot and is it now being written or prepared? I have it on pretty good authority that such is the case. If it is the case, I am sure you must be in the know.

And what do you think—I don't expect you to answer this question—of those who protest their pious loyalty to a great man's dying wishes (in public) at the same time preparing (in private) to controvert those wishes in exactly the same manner—but to a much greater extent—that I had planned to; for which presumption they had roused their whole small establishment to indignation and suspicion against me? Yours for pious perfidy in high church places,

April 9, [1971]

Dearest Frances: Three things: (1) Will you send me my piece on Whittaker Chambers (from that slew of stuff called <u>Angels Unaware</u> which I <u>think</u> you have.)

(2) Can you check Ezra Pound's US sales? (see my letter of March 15 or thereabouts.)

(3) Telephone me at 1 p.p. New York time either April 15 or 17—after you've mulled over the following report, slept on it, simmered down, and come to some sort of conclusion?

We've been Pearl Harboured. Three days ago I had a drink with my friend James Fawcett of Chatham House, a former All Souls' Fellow, at ask his advice about those Vivienne Eliot papers "in Bodley". James said he would ask his friend John Bell of the Oxford Press what the proper procedure would be. The next day he wrote me as follows:

'I have spoken to John Bell; he knows about the Eliot papers in the Bodleian, and of your interest in them, as says that it is a 'very delicate' situation, In particular, he says: (1) a biography of Eliot is being written for Faber & Faber. They would not want to see the Bodleian papers in the hands of a competing biographer. Helen Gardner, though not the author of the biography, is involved here; (2) The second wife is editing Eliot's letters and would try to stop any disclosure of the Bodleian papers to anyone else.

'He thinks that there are only two possible courses: (a) An APPROACH TO Fabers to get an agreed common use of the Bodleian papers; or (b) A direct letter to Robert Shackleton, Bodley's Librarian, asking for access to the papers, given the terms of the bequest. He doubts whether (a) would work. I know Charles Monteith well, a director of Fabers, and he might be approached if you think it worth while.

'I am sorry to have achieved so little.

'We look forward very much to seeing you again. Yours ever,'.

I told James to hold his horses, but to try to find out from Monteith who the biographer is, and when Faber expects to publish the book.

I have written (but not sent) a stinger to Frank Morley, who must have been in the know from the start—whenever that was—ending 'Yours for pious perfidy in high church places.'

Well? The count being two and three in the ninth, and no outs, Charlie Brown and Schroeder (isn't he the catcher?) had better have a conference. Don't you think?

A letter dated April 5th, 1971

Dear Tom: I have just got back from Australia to find two messages from Joyce Weiner. The first is to the effect that she is retiring and I am very sorry to hear this. Secondly, she says that you would now like me to take some action about persuading the Bodleian to release some of the Eliot papers to you. I know that we discussed this but I have in fact forgotten exactly what I said I would do. If you would be good enough to refresh my memory I will do it at once! Yours ever, Alan (A. D. Maclean, of Macmillans).

April 9, [1971]

Dear Alan: Welcome back up on top. Yes it's very sad about Joyce Weiner. But the doctors say she has to, so I'm sure she'll make the best of it.

I can't remember what you were supposed to do about the Bodleian either—short of getting those damn papers for me. But the situation is even more ticklish now, so I won't ask you to do anything at the moment, except have lunch. Or would you like to join Christopher Sykes and me for dinner on April 21? Love to have you, but if you'd rather make it lunch, what about Wednesday the 28th?
Yours ever,

April 14, [1971]

(1) VALERIE, DU SAUTOY & Co. have decided to scrap their noble but untenable position of upholding T. S. ELIOT's dying wish that no biography of him should be written, and to beat the opposition to the draw by getting out their own biography first. Unlike their earlier and opposite stand, this decision is secret. The biographer's name and the proposed publication date are also secret.

(2) They will continue their (apparently but no longer) dog-in-the-manger policy of refusing access to all unpublished papers and refusing permission to quote from published but copyright works. "The family will no co-operate either"—nor friends.

What I must do:

(1) Speed up (it would not be fatal to them to bring out their book after mine; but it would be fatal for me to bring out mine after theirs.)

(2) If possible, force them to let me see and use copyright material—i.e. Have the law on them.

(3) Keep them in the dark about my intentions as long as possible; that is, until I'm ready to act.

(JOHN Bell—of the Oxford Press—as reported by James Fawcett): "He thinks that there are only two possible courses: (a) an approach to Fabers to get an agreed common use of the Bodleian papers; or (b) a direct letter to ROBERT SHACKLETON,

Bodley's Librarian, asking for access to the papers, given the terms of the bequest. He doubts whether (a) would work."

But I want access to more than the Bodleian papers: I want access to the papers at the Houghton Library, the University of Texas, and King's College, Cambridge. And I wasn't permission to quote from these and from published works. None of these things will be forthcoming unless I can force them by law.

April 15, [1971]

It doesn't look good. Yesterday I rang COLIN OLIVER, my solicitor, to tell him the latest development, and ask him what, if anything, I could do legally to get the papers from the Bodleian, and in general. He said he would take counsel with the copyright expert, and ring me back, which he did last evening. And the gist of his report is that apparently nothing can be done. Legally they seem to have me over a barrel.

When I asked him what their moral position was, and whether I couldn't make them feel rotten about that, he said, "Yes, in the newspapers for a day or so." I asked him if he was being a little cynical about Faber & Faber, who were supposed to be the very moral top of the publishing world. He said he didn't have much opinion of the morality of publishers, having had experience of it.

I have yet to hear from FRANCES LINDLEY, who should ring me tonight from New York, or possibly the day after tomorrow. I've been trying to think things over to see what there is to be done, and as yet I can't think, except that if there is to be a book written by me, it will have to be written a good deal faster that I had planned or hoped to write it. And trying to imagine what the point of view of the opposition is, I think I can understand it as far as their attitude towards me is concerned. I am either completely unknown, or if know at all, either not considered to be qualified, or considered not to be qualified, to write a book on ELIOT. Well, if PHILIP MAIRET is right in saying that if I were the right man to do such a book I would know it, then certainly I am not the right man, because I don't know it.

I have just written a letter, but haven't sent it yet, to MRS. ELIOT.

> Dear Mrs. Eliot: Although you did not acknowledge my last letter (Dec. 12, 1970) I am writing you once again, to ask you to grant me an audience.
>
> At this point, I think, it would be to both our interests to meet and try to agree on a course of action—or decide not to agree! But I believe that the progress of our common interest has now reached a stage where some clarification is needed.
>
> If you would be kind enough to denote a place and time for our meeting, I will try to suit your convenience. I should of course not object to a member of the firm of Faber & Faber also being present; and in that case I should expect to bring with me my own legal counsel. Yours sincerely,

I am now going to try to telephone COLIN OLIVER and ask him what he thinks about sending this letter.

April 16, [1971]

FRANCES LINDLEY telephoned from New York last night as I had asked her to do, and I'm afraid our conference was a CHARLIE BROWN affair—but with no clarifying tag-line. She wanted me to get JAMES FAWCETT to play a much more active role on my behalf than I am sure he is willing to play; and she seemed to feel that the best thing to do would be to have a conference with Faber & Faber and put it to them that their thing was to share and share alike. I can't quite see Faber seeing it that way. She agreed that it might be well to get my book finished before the official biography, but didn't hazard any guess about how soon I should get it done; and kept saying that, after all, this would be a book about ELIOT's years in the United States. This is not my idea of the book, and besides, I doubt very much if I could get any original stuff on his years in the United States, the first seventeen of his life. The gist of her advise was to be of good cheer, and just keep on keeping on. I think my next step will be to go and see JOYCE WEINER in London, and see if she can give me any more usable advice.

April 17, [1971]

A letter from COLIN OLIVER, dated 16 April:

> This is a time of year when counsel are not in chambers because the Easter vacation does not end until Monday. Through his clerk, however, I managed to track down Mr. William Aldous, an expert in copyright matters, at his country house, and had a telephone conference. I made sure that he has never acted for the literary executors of T. S. Eliot or, for that matter, Eliot himself, and told him that your interest in writing a biography had led to a resistance on the part of the literary executors, not only in refusing their own co-operation but in instigating a clam-like policy with King's College, Cambridge, and Harvard and Texas Universities.
> His advice was not particularly cheering. If the copyright in Eliot's published works in his unpublished papers belongs to the literary executors, the reproduction of any substantial part of any of those works or papers without their permission is a breach of copyright, and if it came to their knowledge that substantial parts of his works were about to be published, the Court in this country has power to grant an injunction to prevent the infringement, or further infringements, if some have

already occurred. His advice, therefore, was that if your book depends on substantial quotation from Eliot, it would be necessary to obtain permission from his literary executors, who are free either to withhold their permission to grant it subject to conditions. Normally the condition is payment, but, if your information that Fabers are planning an opposition biography is correct, they may just refuse permission.

On the subject of the Eliot papers left to the Bodleian by his fist wife, Counsel suggested that I should look at a copy of her Will to ascertain whether she had merely left the papers to the Bodleian or whether she had also given the copyright. If there was any express gift of the copyright in her will, it might now reside either in her executors or, in the case of papers written by Eliot himself, in his literary executors. In either case, the same fifty-year rule would apply to reproducing them in print.

The other point which Counsel made was that, so far as the law of copyright is concerned, there is no reason why the Bodleian, King's or either of the American universities should refuse you access to the papers for the purpose of reading them, and if they hedge on the ground that there is some legal impediment in showing them to you, that must exist for some other reason. I think the most likely reason is that they regard themselves as bound by contract, either because they have accepted the papers from the literary executors on condition that they keep them secret for a period or have entered into some express arrangement to that effect. Whether such an agreement is binding on them could be a nice legal question, but getting hold of them at all could tempt a librarian to agree to all sorts of conditions which might later appear silly or unnecessary. It would be worth exploring with the respective curators, their ground for the statement or belief that they cannot show them to you.

Counsel also suggested that, if possible, you should come to some accommodation with the literary executors in case, without that, there could be too little quotation in your book to give it the necessary ring of Eliot. He agreed that if your research is now well advanced it would obviously be better to publish your book before theirs arrives, but the fact that you are at least many months ahead of any author they engage, might give you some leverage in discussion. I agree with the proposal which you made over the telephone this morning that it would be a good thing to meet Valerie and her co-executors, try to find out why she has been so unco-operative, and test the possibility of wider co-operation. Perhaps they have not yet chosen an author, and what better result could be achieved than that your book should be published by Fabers here and Harper & Row in the States? If I can be any use in helping to organize the meeting, for example, by talking to Jabez-Smith, I should be very pleased to do so, but if you can keep lawyers out of the first meeting I believe that would be better.

April 20, [1971]

I finally heard from MARQUIS CHILDS, a newspaper correspondent, formerly of the St. Louis <u>Post Dispatch</u>, whom I had written to on the 5th November, but never heard from; so I wrote again on April 13, asking him if he knew ELIOT during his St. Louis days, or if he knew <u>of</u> him and his family, and if so, whether he'd be willing to write me a paragraph of reminiscence. The gist of his letter was that he'd been travelling during a good bit of his time, and therefore hadn't answered my letter. "I did not know ELIOT except for one occasion when I lunched with him when he was active in Faber & Faber, the firm that published my book, Sweden, the Middle Way. I have no recollection of this encounter except for his quality of gentleness, almost shyness.

At some point in the early '30s when I was still in St. Louis with the <u>Post Dispatch</u>, his father was Chancellor of the University at that time. (His father was no such thing; his grandfather had been Chancellor of the University but that was long before he was born.)

"Have you written to THOMAS S. ELIOT [Initial should be 'H'], the current Chancellor who's about to retire and who was, I think, a cousin of T. S.? He might be able to supply you with a copy of that letter and also to give you much more information. He is a friend and a very fine human being who has gone through hell with the student demonstrations out there."

April 21, [1971]

Went to London, and went to see JOYCE WEINER, my agent, who has just retired, and showed her the file of letters on the latest developments. She too, like FRANCES LINDLEY, refused to be downhearted, said I was having a wonderful time, and: "Press on!" One suggestion she did make was that we might invite VALERIE ELIOT down to Cavendish for a weekend, on the grounds that she would be so captivated by the surroundings there that she would completely surrender. Her sister Marjorie gave me a couple of leads; one about a Brother Basil Cunningham, at Portsmouth Priory, Rhode Island, whose real name is THOMAS STEARNS—which seems promising. And the other one, a man named SCHUTE, who worked with ELIOT on Murder in the Cathedral. She says she can arrange to have me meet both of these gentlemen.

I then went off to lunch with JOYCE's successor, MRS. DAVID OWEN, at Buck's. I found her very personable, and alert. She asked me about what I had written, and for the rest of the hour-and-a-half I'm afraid she didn't get a word in edgewise. She had heard no rumours about the official biography of ELIOT, but said she would check around with various people, and see what she would find out.

That evening I had dinner with CHRISTOPHER SYKES, also at Buck's. We had a couple of drinks in the bar beforehand, with LORD COLYTON (I can't even spell it—I used to know him as HENRY HOPKINSON, who married ALICE ENO); and afterwards CHRISTOPHER and I had dinner alone. I wish to heaven I had been able to get him down on tape. I took what notes I could, but they are feeble compared to what he said. He was very co-operative, and said that if there were anything more he could do or tell me, he'd certainly be very glad to; and we made a tentative date for him to come down to Cavendish when he has finished his book on NANCY ASTOR, which he says should be some time in July. So that after we get back from the States I hope to get him down, and perhaps he can fill in some of the yawning gaps in my notes. Here's what they are for the moment:

> Sykes's first meeting with Eliot was, he thinks, some time in 1957, shortly after the death of Vivienne; and he met him at the flat which I think, by then, Eliot shared with Hayward. Sykes remembered that he was carrying a bowler, and seemed very conservative. Sykes had gone to see Hayward, and Eliot came in carrying his bowler.
>
> Then, when he came on subsequent visits, Hayward would say: "Do call in on the Bard before you go." (He always called him "the Bard" or "my lodger".) And Sykes would have a few words.
>
> Apparently Evelyn Waugh admired Eliot from afar, and wanted to meet him. (They didn't, in fact,

ever meet.) When Sykes told Eliot what he called
"a very funny story" about Waugh and Lord Charles
Cavendish, Eliot gave Sykes a close look, "and
I could see that we might be friends." He put it
slightly differently a minute later. He said: "Eliot
glared at me." (And they were very close friends
after that.)

SYKES had a profounder feeling for ELIOT than for
HAYWARD. The last time SYKES saw HAYWARD, about six months
before he died. HAYWARD hoped that he could have a meeting
with ELIOT, but they were both too ill. On the telephone to
SYKES, HAYWARD said that he wouldn't go to the Abbey memorial
service for ELIOT, which SYKES seemed to feel he might well
have done.
 He said that VALERIE had every reason to hate him
(HAYWARD). And ELIOT knew, according to SYKES, that HAYWARD
was the most colossal gossip in London. SYKES says: "I've
never met such a gossip as HAYWARD in my life."
 The true story of ELIOT's breaking the news to HAYWARD
that he was going to get married to VALERIE, I got from
SYKES, who got it straight from HAYWARD, apparently. And it
wasn't true that ELIOT left a note for him, because "with the
cowardice of a sensitive man" he was afraid to face HAYWARD.
He didn't leave a note for him, saying that he wouldn't be in
for breakfast tomorrow because he was getting married. This
is SYKES's version:

> On the morning that Eliot left, about six o'clock, he
> came into Hayward's room and said: I've got to go away,
> and I want you to read this. Then Eliot have him a
> letter.
> Hayward says: All night, I'll read the thing.
> Aren't you going to read it now?
> Yes, but...
> But you ought to read it now.

Hayward reads it then says: Well, that's fine, but why didn't you tell me?

Oh, because I thought you might be angry.

My dear old Tom, I couldn't be angry with you.

Then Eliot leans forward, takes him in his arms and kisses him, saying: Oh, I knew I could always rely on you.

Hayward said later, Coming the most un-homosexual man in London, I found this a most offensive gesture.

The housekeeper, whose following remarks SYKES reports, was a Frenchwoman. (I think they had several, but this must have been at the time when, before ELIOT married, she looked after them very nicely.) She said: "Vous trouvez ici le veuf joyeux? Ah, ca, non!"

(The following comment, in SYKES's own words, was added when he visited Cavendish; see p. &&&):

On the day TSE got married I was producing in a BBC studio. I saw the news in a copy of The Evening Standard. I immediately rang up Hayward to ask if the story was true. He said it was and I said I would come to his rooms as soon as my rehearsal was over.

When I arrived I found Noel Blakiston there as well. He had just arrived. AS the French housekeeper left the room she made the remark about 'le veuf joyeux'. Hayward then told us the story exactly as you have recorded. If the story was otherwise I cannot see how the kissing incident could come in. Hayward was so embittered that later he invented versions more to TSE's discredit.

After hearing the story Noel B, who never knew TSE, probed a little further. He asked is TSE had left Hayward in the lurch as regards rent. Hayward said that, knowing that it might take a long time to get a new lodger, TSE had paid him in rent covering two years. Then not very seriously Noel B. asked is TSE was homosexual. Haywards answered Good Heavens NO. We all laughed. Noel B summed up and said:

When I asked Sykes: "Which did you like better, of Eliot and Hayward?" he refused to choose, and said very emphatically: "Both!" I said: "How well did you feel you knew Eliot?" Sykes said: "Not profoundly." But it seems to me that he knew him pretty well.

When I asked him: "Did you agree with Hayward that Yeats was Eliot's superior as a poet?" he seemed to think it might be an open question, but I think his nearest reply was something like: "We-ell, Mm-m-m..."

On the day TSE got married I was producing in a BBC studio. I saw the news in a copy of <u>The Evening Standard</u>. I immediately rang up Hayward to ask if the story was true. He said it was and I said I would come to his rooms as soon as my rehearsal was over.

When I arrived I found Noel Blakiston there as well. He had just arrived. As the French housekeeper left the room she made the remark about 'le veuf joyeux'. Hayward then told us the story exactly as you have recorded. If the story was otherwise I cannot see how the kissing incident could come in. Hayward was so embittered that later he invented versions more to TSE's discredit.

After hearing the story Noel B, who never knew TSE, probed a little further. He asked is TSE had left Hayward in the lurch as regards rent. Hayward said that, knowing that it might take a long time to get a new lodger, TSE had paid him in rent covering two years. Then not very seriously Noel B. asked is TSE was homosexual. Haywards answered Good Heavens NO. We all laughed. Noel B summed up and said: "Then it looks to me as if nothing wrong has been done" or words to that effect. Hayward appeared to agree.

The last incident of the evening was when Noel B asked if TSE's room was still as it had been. Hayward said it was and I took Noel B to see it.

(Sykes is going to let me see photographs of himself, Eliot and Hayward outside the Church of St. Thomas More.)

After Eliot left him, Hayward decided to act well, and at first did. Sykes says he and Eliot pushed Hayward around Battersea Park when the weather was fine, and around the gardens of the Chelsea Hospital in winter, I think, for <u>ten years</u>.

After Vivienne's death, Eliot was avoiding everybody, and Hayward said that her death was shattering. Eliot told him, between his tears: "I've not got a single second of happiness to look back on, and that makes it worse."

According to Sykes, Eliot and he had "a comic relationship".

Eliot and Waugh were apparently mutually fascinated with each other, and kept sending messages through Hayward. As Sykes put it:

"A great deal of flirting went on."

Eliot and Hayward always came to lunch on Christmas with Sykes. One Christmas, Eliot a bit tight, swooped hats with Sykes, who said: "My dear Bard, this hat is too small for me." Eliot said: "Oh well, my brain only works part of the time."

He told me an anecdote about "Madame Supercargo", as they called her, (she was the Chilean Ambassador's wife) "an idiot of the first water,"—and Eliot adored her. She kept saying: "Ah, Tom, you will read us one of your poems!" And then he did.

Eliot said to Sykes, when told that Madame Supercargo had said to him (Sykes): "What do you do when you don't write?" and he said could lack of nothing to my, so she said "Don't time hand heavy on your hands?", (Again he could think of nothing) – You should have said," Eliot told him, "When I do write, the time hands heavy on my hands."

Alas, that's the extent of my notes. I wish, as I say, I had it on tape, but there was much more that I missed.

I posted the letter to Valerie. I'm not sure whether I recorded that or not, so perhaps I'd better do that again.

April 21, 1971

Dear Mrs. Eliot: Although you did not acknowledge my last letter (Dec. 12, 1970) I am writing you once again, to ask you to grant me an audience.

At this point, I think, it would be to both our interest to meet and try to agree on a course of action—or decide not to agree! But I believe that our common concern has now reached a stage where some clarification is needed.

If you would be kind enough to denote a place and time for such a meeting, I will try to suit your convenience. Yours sincerely,

I don't expect an answer to that, but if I don't get one within a reasonably length of time I've decided to write to PETER DU SAUTOY, who is, I think, the head of the firm of Faber & Faber, and who wrote an open letter to the Press, obviously in answer to my letter which asked all and sundry to send me anything they had on ELIOT. DU SAUTOY's letter said, in effect, that they, as ELIOT's old friends and publishers, were going to honour his wishes, and so I'm going to try to smoke him out. In the meantime, I've asked PAT GARRATT, my researcher, to look up his letter (unfortunately I didn't keep a copy of it) and send me a Xerox of it. I told her, perhaps the quickest way of finding out when it was published, or getting a copy of the text, was to telephone to his secretary. "But," I said, "for heaven's sake, don't mention my name, and if they ask you who you're representing, just say you're working for a firm called 'Ding Dong Bell'!" I had a vague feeling that came into one of Shakespeare's songs in which he uses the word "forsworn", and that DU SAUTOY might either get the reference or feel there was something sinister about it!

I should also write letters to MUNBY, of the King's College Library, and to Boyd (or whatever his name is), the head of the Houghton Library at Harvard, and to the librarian at the University of Texas. These letters all to be vetted by COLIN OLIVER, my solicitor, but quoting his copyright authority, and asking by what legal right do they refuse me access to the papers in their ELIOT collections.

The Bodleian papers is a separate problem in a way; I have had no more word from JAMES FAWCETT about anything in that direction, and I'm very loath to try to enlist the services of JOHN SPARROW, because I personally don't like him, and because he was an enemy of ELIOT's. I did have an idea, if I wanted to make a stink about it in public, perhaps it would be a good idea to tell the whole story to RICHARD CROSSMAN, to see what the New Statesman could do. Or, perhaps, to BERNARD LEVIN, who now writes a column in The Times. That's something to think about.

In the meantime, the broken reed that BILL DEAKIN recommended to me, MR. D. M. DAVIN, of The Clarendon Press, who seems to me strongly to resemble Chicundra, the Water Rat, has now written that he can't even have a drink with us on Tuesday next, when we go down to Oxford for an Ashmolean expedition, because he has a financial meeting that afternoon. So I think I'll write him off.

Incidentally, on the 22nd April I was going into the London Library, and just about a hundred yards from it ran smack into BILL DEAKIN himself, who gave me a very bad news about his wife, PUSSY; but when I told him about DAVIN, and how feeble he had been, he said he would think about it, and see if he couldn't find somebody who would be more help.

April 24, 1971

This morning, a letter from VALERIE ELIOT, dated 22nd April:

> Dear Mr. Matthews: I must apologise for my delay in thanking you for your letter of December 12th but at the time I was under some pressure preparing a manuscript for the Press, while handicapped by a broken arm.
> It was thoughtful of you to point out these errors in To Criticise the Critic. As a matter of fact we had already noticed them and, alas, several others. I find nowadays that no sooner has one caught one lot of errors than a second crop appears. Yours sincerely, Valerie Eliot. P.S. Since dictating the above to my part-time secretary last Monday, and receiving it today, the 23rd, your letter of the 21st has come. I am afraid there really is no point in a meeting. You knew the position at the outset and yet chose to go ahead against my husband's wishes. My own feelings do not come into the matter. As the executrix I am bound to carry out his instructions not 'to facilitate or countenance' the writing of a biography. V. E.

April 28, [1971]

Lunch with ALAN MACLEAN of MACMILLANS, at Brook's, and told him what the present situation was. He said the only thing he could suggest about getting the Bodleian papers was to get the University Chancellor to work on it, which he was rather loath to attempt, the Chancellor being old HAROLD MACMILLAN, his boss. So I said, "Oh no, no, I wouldn't think of that." He congratulated me on my optimism but seemed to think it odd, and he himself didn't seem to share my optimism, and he seemed to think that the only two possible ways out for me would be (a) for Faber & Faber to switch from whatever biographer they were thinking of employing, to me, which we both thought very unlikely; and (b) to have me change from writing a biography to writing a critical book, and then applying to VALERIE ELIOT for the forbidden papers. And in that case, we both agreed that she wouldn't trust me, and also that's not the book I set out to write. Anyway, he said he would check with PETER DU SAUTOY of Fabers, and ask him directly about the truth of this report that they were bringing out a biography; and he would telephone me this afternoon or the following. Well, he didn't telephone me that afternoon, not the following morning—at least so far. But JAMES FAWCETT did, and he had asked his friend, CHARLES MONTEITH, a Director of Fabers. MONTEITH had told him: "No, no book." And he thinks that his friend, JOHN BELL, whom he is going to see again later today, had got things muddled up on account of the T. S. ELIOT letters VALERIE ELIOT is bringing out.

So perhaps that's the end of that rumour.

Draft of a letter to PETER DU SAUTOY, Managing Director of Faber & Faber. (I haven't sent this letter, and I may not send it; certainly, I probably won't send it in this draft, but here is the draft):

> Dear Mr. Du Sautoy: Because you (with T. S. Eliot's executor) are the custodian of a bequest whose absurdity I am only one of the first to point out – and the many who come after me will prove to be overwhelming, as I think you will hardly

deny – seems to me as insufficient reason for us not to meet. We have a common problem, and I don't imagine that either of us is altogether satisfied that the present impasse is the best available solution.

If we do meet, as I hope we shall – and will, if you will agree to it – I don't for a moment suggest that it can or should alter either of our positions. I am sanguine enough to hope, however, that a meeting between us might not only clear the air (which seems to me to be getting a little overcharged) but also might go some way, at least, toward clarifying our common problem. If you agree that we have one!

"As you know, T. S. ELIOT himself changed his mind on this subject in the last few years of his life, or else was unaware of the discrepancy between the memorandum he attached to his Will and the sentiments he had expressed in 1956 (On Poetry and Poets):

'I do suggest that the personality and the private life a dead poet constitutes sacred ground on which the psychologist must not tread. The scientist must be at liberty to study such material as his curiosity leads him to investigate – as long as the victim is dead and the laws of libel cannot be invoked to stop him. Nor is there any reason why the biographies of poets should not be written.'

While I was writing this letter, Alan Maclean rang up to report a conversation he had just had with you. When I told him I was hoping to get you to agree to a meeting, he said he thought it unlikely that you would consent. I am sending this letter nevertheless, in the hope that he may be mistaken. Yours sincerely,

April 29, [1971]

To COLIN OLIVER, Esq., Bircham & Co., 1 Dean Farrar Street, London, S.W.1.

>Dear Colin: The report that Faber & Faber were quietly planning an opposition biography turned out to be a false alarm. I suppose that's good news but it doesn't get us any forwarder with the forbidden Eliot papers.
>
>I'm enclosing, for your patient perusal and advice, a draft of a letter to the three Librarians principally concerned. I not only want your criticisms and suggestions on the letter itself but your opinion on whether I should send it now or wait for a possibly more favourable moment.
>
>We're looking forward to seeing all Olivers or as many as possible either on the 15th or the 29th. Yours ever,

(And the enclosure): To Dr. A. L. Munby, Librarian, King's College, Cambridge: Mr. W. H. Bond, Librarian, The Houghton Library, Harvard University, Cambridge, Mass.: Mrs. Mary Hirth, Academic Centre Librarian, University of Texas, Austin, Texas:

>Dear Blank: This letter is written with the knowledge and consent of my solicitors, Bircham & Company, of 1 Dean Farrar Street, London, S.W.1.
>
>I am informed that under the law of copyright there is no reason why any library should refuse me access to any T. S. Eliot papers in their possession, for the purpose of reading such papers (the right of publishing quotations from them being a different matter).
>
>Since you have refused me access to certain Eliot papers in your library, you must feel yourself bound by some extra-legal agreement. Will you be kind enough to tell me what that agreement is? Yours sincerely, T. S. Matthews.

April 30, [1971]

JAMES FAWCETT just rang from London to tell me that he had seen JOHN BELL, of the Oxford Press, yesterday, and it turns out that he has misunderstood what BELL told him. BELL had said, apparently, not that Faber had actually undertaken an opposition biography but that they would very probably be forced to it by people like me, if they kept up this way. But so far, at least, there's no plan.

Just had a telephone call from ALAN MACLEAN, who had talked to PETER DU SAUTOY, and he says the same thing; at present they have absolutely no plans for an official biography, but he does think—he gave ALAN the impression he thought perhaps in a year or so they would be forced into it by people like me. When I told ALAN that I am, at present, writing a letter to DU SAUTOY, suggesting a meeting between him an me, he said that he didn't think that DU SAUTOY would see me, or that it would accomplish anything. I just said: "Well, when I get my letter written, I'll speak it into this record."

I've also just had a letter from Colin Oliver:

April 29. Dear Tom: Many thanks for your letter of the 20th April sending me a copy of Vivienne Eliot's Will. I have an idea we shall get stuck again because in addition to the two brothers of T. S. Eliot (you will know if they are still in the land of the living) she also appointed St. John Hutchinson, Geoffrey Faber and Philip Morrel, as her executors. As I read the bequest to the Bodleian contained in Clause 5 of her Will, the property and the papers there mentioned vested in the Bodleian, but her executors would, under the general law, retain the copyright in any of her original writings and I suppose T. S. Eliot's executors retain copyright in any letters or other writings of his which she included in her bequest to the Bodleian.

> I do not know St. John Hutchinson or Philip
> Morrell and Geoffrey Faber we can, I assume, write
> off as being on the other side. It hardly looks as
> though a direct approach to the executors would
> help with the Bodleian papers or any others, but I
> could discover the name of the firm of solicitors
> who extracted Vivienne's probate and make an
> approach through them, if you would like me to do
> so. For that matter I would also be willing to make
> an approach to Jabez-Smith of Herbert Oppenheimers.
> I knew him well at one time but it is some years
> since I have seen him and he will probably remember
> me only if we meet.
>   I am sorry that my advice seems to lack
> ingenuity in discovering new ways of extracting
> copyright material, but perhaps by now you
> have organized a direct approach to his widow.
> Yours sincerely, Colin.

ALAN said that he heard that the candidates for the official biography were already queuing up.

May 1, [1971]

This looks like a slight break at last. A letter from STEWART C. SHERMAN, John Hay Librarian, Brown University Library, April 28.

> Dear Mr. Matthews: In reply to your letter of April
> 19th the John Hay Library does have a copy of Notes on
> the Early Life of T. S. Eliot by H. W. H. Powell, Jr., an
> unpublished dissertation. You would be most welcome
> to have access to it here in the library, during your
> visit this coming summer.
>   You will find this in the University archives in
> the John Hay Library. Sincerely yours.

May 1, [1971]

JOYCE WEINER tells me that COMPTON MACKENZIE has said that BERTRAND RUSSELL seduced VIVIENNE ELIOT, and that COMPTON MACKENZIE is never wrong about these things.

May 8, [1971]

This morning, with my Wimbledon tickets, I got a note from PETER DU SAUTOY, the Chairman of Faber & Faber:

> 5th May, Dear Mr. Matthews: Thank you for your letter of May 1st. Of course I shall be very glad to see you (without prejudice, as they say); please let me know you are likely to be in London. Yours sincerely, Peter Du Sautoy.

The next time I'm planning to be in London is on a Bank Holiday. I'm going to give him a choice of two dates: Monday, May 31, or Wednesday, June 9.
A letter from COLIN OLIVER:

> Dear Tom: Thank you for your letter of the 29th April enclosing the draft of a letter to the three librarians. The draft contains all the essential material but would not, I believe, produce the desired results. I enclose an alternative draft for your consideration. It is longer, but I have tried to bring out in it the fact the copyright is a matter which we can handle with the literary executors but that the production of the papers for you to read is entirely a matter for the librarian (of his governing body) and, if they are to make excuses, we shall not listen to anything about copyright. There is no magic in the words I have used – but perhaps you will in the end write something between your draft and mine. Yours ever, Colin.

And this is the draft letter to librarians having custody of T. S. ELIOT papers:

Dear Blank: You may recollect that last year I told you that I was writing a biography of T. S. Eliot and asked you to give me access to the Eliot papers in the custody of your library for the purposes of my research. At that time, and, I believe, without reference to any body of persons governing the library, you refused to show me those papers, ostensibly on the ground that the copyright did not vest in the library. On this question I have taken legal advice and the opinion which I have received establishes, to my mind beyond doubt, that the law of copyright cannot afford you any valid ground for refusing me access to the papers so that I can read them and form my own conclusion about their contents as part of my research for a serious work of scholarship. I and my advisers are perfectly aware that if, having completed that research, I should wish to quote the whole or any substantial part of the papers which I have read, I should need to obtain the consent of the owner of the copyright, but if your library is not owner of the copyright, that is quite another question which in no way affects my present application to have access to those papers for the sole purpose of reading them.

I should be grateful if you would let me know when I may arrange to call to study the T. S. Eliot collection in your custody. But if, after full consideration of this letter, you and any trustees or other governing body to whom you refer are minded to reject my present request, please state the ground upon which you claim to be inhibited from producing them to me. Yours, etc..

Well, this seems a bit harsh and legal in the language to me, and I think the sharp edges don't quite fit the slight differences in the three librarians; but it certainly has the gist of it and I'm going to use this as the basis for a letter that I'll send out myself.

* * *

[page begins here] instigators of the whole horrid plot) and Macmillans of London (who are tagging along to the extent of having taken an option on the book).

"And I shall await MR. HOBSON's report with what patience I can summon. Yours ever, TOM".

May 12, [1971]

A letter received dated May 10, 1971

> Dear Mr. Matthews: Mr. Du Sautoy has asked me to thank you for your letter of May 8th and to say the he will be pleased to see you here on Wednesday June 9th at 10.30 a.m. I hope this will be convenient for you. Yours sincerely, Mavis. E. Pindard, Secretary to Mr. Peter Du Sautoy.

May 12, [1971]

> Dear Miss Pindard: Thank you for your letter of May 10. Please tell Mr. Du Sautoy that I shall be delighted to come to his office at 10.30 a.m. on Wednesday, June 9. Yours sincerely, T. S. Matthews."

May 14, 1971 (from Colin Oliver)

> Dear Tom: We shall be able to talk about your meeting with Peter Du Sautoy when we come to Cavendish but I

see that the first date that you offer him, 31st May, is Whit Monday, and I doubt whether he will be in his office then.

Without mentioning any names, I asked Anthony Hobson – who is Sotheby's manuscript man – what he would do if the Bodleian refused to produce their Eliot papers.

He knows Shackleton very well indeed and is himself co-operating with one of the Bodleian people in the production of a book. He tells me that if my client – that is you – is willing to disclose his name and the name of the publishers, and tells him exactly what he wants to see, he would try to raise it in conversation en passant when next in Oxford. Yours ever, Colin.

May 17, [1971]

"COLIN OLIVER Esq., Bircham & Co.:

Dear Colin: Thank you for your letter of May 14. If your friend, Mr. Anthony Hobson, would indeed speak to Mr. Shackleton when he is next in Oxford, I am quite willing to disclose my name (T. S. Matthews is the pseudonym I generally use) and the names of my publishers: Harper & Row in New York (the 'prejudice.' That's to be on June 9.

In the Bodleian confrontation no one is so much as blinking. The friend of a friend, who is supposed to know Shackleton (the Bodleian Librarian) very well is to have 'a quiet word' with him about me, next time he goes to Oxford. What will come of that, knows God.

Plans for my summer trip to the States have now firmed up. The France should land me in New York July 14 (Pam's flying over later; I meet her in Boston on the

18th). I head immediately for Baltimore (John Hopkins ear clinic – and a new buzzer, I hope); the only time I've allotted to New York is August 9, 10 and 11 – we sail at midnight on the 11th.

If Texas capitulates I go there, of course. Ditto Harvard. I've arranged to see at Brown an unpublished dissertation on Eliot's youth and early years; also his cousin and my old friend, Mrs. Sturtevant, in Newport – another delicate situation, but I hope she'll show me her photograph album, at least. In New England I hope to see Conrad Aiken, Edmund Wilson, Archie MacLeish and possibly Donald Gallup.

Try to save us a night for dinner, of those three I named.

May 15, [1971]

A letter from the Librarian, The Houghton Library, Harvard University, Cambridge, Mass., 15 May, 1971.

> Dear Mr. Matthews: I have your letter of May 11 concerning the T. S. Eliot collection in this library.
> I am afraid that there has been some misunderstanding of our position. We did not refuse access 'on the grounds that copyright did not vest in the library,' although, as you are evidently aware, copyright on all unpublished manuscript of Eliot is vested in Mrs. Eliot as his heir.
> We refused access to you, as we have to other potential biographers of Eliot, out of co-operation with Mrs. Eliot, who has worked with us (as did her late husband and his brother) in augmenting and perfecting our collection. It is in very large part a family collection. We therefore feel bound in simple courtesy to consult Mrs. Eliot about potential users of the

collection, and to abide by her decisions. The grounds
for such decisions are her own. If you can persuade
Mrs. Eliot that you should be allowed access to the
collection, with or without the additional permission
to excerpt or make direct quotation, we will be glad
to place the papers at your disposal. But in view of an
agreement of long standing, several times reiterated, I
am afraid I must have her consent in writing.

Ours is a library with extensive manuscript
holdings in many fields, most of which are readily
available to scholars without undue formality.
But some of those collections would not be here, or
would cease to received additions of invaluable
material, unless we agreed to various restrictive
stipulations by donors and by families or literary
executors. Persons considering the gift of papers
and collections would not entrust them to us if we
were not known for the careful observance of such
undertakings. The Eliot papers are not alone in this
respect. Very truly yours, W. H. Bond.

How sweetly reasonable; how grown-up. How bad and childish this makes me feel.

May 21, [1971]

The other day I was going through my correspondence files and I came across a letter from the Librarian of McMaster University in Hamilton, Ontario, listing the ELIOT material they had, and I saw what I had missed on my first go round. Halfway down the list was this item: "Undated, 1 November 1921, three letters to B. R. from VIVIEN." The last paragraph of the Librarian's letter said:

> There are no conditions regarding permission
> to research in the Russell archives. Mrs. Eliot's

permission is necessary for the obtaining of
facsimile copies of T. S. Eliot's letters.

So I wrote to MR. BLACKWELL, May 14.

> Dear Mr. Blackwell: You were kind enough to
> send me on September 18, 1970, a list of the T. S.
> Eliot material in your archives. You also said in
> your letter: 'There are no conditions regarding
> permission to research in the Russell archives. Mrs.
> Eliot's permission is necessary for the obtaining of
> facsimile copies of T. S. Eliot's letters.
> I hope this means that it is possible for me to
> obtain copies of some of the other material in your
> list. I should be very happy to pay the cost of photo-
> copying and posting the following:
> 13 June, 1949 – one reply
> 23 May, 1964 – one reply
> Undated, 1 November, 1921 – three letters to R. S.
> from Vivien. Yours sincerely,

Answer dated May 17 from KENNETH BLACKWELL, Archivist, BERTRAND RUSSELL Archives, McMaster University.

> Dear Mr. Matthews: Thank you for your letter of May 14.
> The 12 June 1949 and 23 May 1964 letters are reproduced
> in Russell's autobiography, Volume III, page 52-3 with
> the letters they answer. I checked the transcriptions
> and found only two small errors which he lists. I am
> sorry I cannot send you copies of Vivien Eliot's letters
> without the permission of someone in authority. I
> realise the importance of or at least the interest
> in Russell's relationship with her and ma therefore
> writing on your behalf to an old friend of Russell's who
> I believe could tell much of the story. I will let you
> know what she says. Yours sincerely, Kenneth Blackwell.

I have so far been able to refrain from answering or going on with this correspondence.

May 25, [1971]

I have now heard from the University of Texas. This morning a letter arrived from the Librarian.

May 21, 1971

>Dear Mr. Matthews; I have re-checked our correspondence concerning the Eliot papers and can find no record of having told you that the Eliot manuscripts are inaccessible. The list I gave you in my letter of July 31, 1970 is complete with one exception which was not catalogues at the time the list was made; that is The Dry Salvages (Les Trois Sauvages) typed manuscript with holography revised version of the last eighteen lines signed and initialled. I might say, too, that the item, The Confidential Clerk, excerpts, three pages, no date, is in the hand of Mary Trevelyan with some holograph comments by her. The only other Eliot manuscript material we have is the letters. Enclosed you will find a copy of a letter dated 14 July, 1970 to Mr. John Hay Iselin from Mr. F. W. Roberts explaining the situation concerning both manuscripts and letters. You will note that he asked if you had discussed with Mrs. Eliot the possibility of having access to the letters without quoting them. I have no indication from you or from Mrs. Eliot that you did this.
>
>Should you wish to examine the manuscripts, I should be pleased to present your request to the Faculty Committee which controls the use of all manuscripts and other unique materials and let you know their decision at the earliest possible

time. I expect no objection since the Committee is always eager to co-operate with legitimate scholars whenever possible. If Mrs. Eliot will give you a letter of which you will send me a photo-copy, or send the letter to me saying she has no objection to your examining the letters that request could also be presented to the Committee.

Mr. Iselin came to the University September 23, 1970 and discussed the situation with me at some length. I believe he also talked with Mr. Roberts. I would suggest again that if you wish to use the letters you get in touch with Mrs. Eliot, tell her what you are doing and ask her permission to examine them and take notes. Sincerely, Mary M. Hirth, Librarian, Academic Centre.

Enclosure to Mr. John Jay Iselin, Vice-President, Harper & Row, Publishers, 49 E. 33rd Street, New York. 14 July, 1970. "Dear Mr. Iselin: Thank you very much for your letter of 10 July about the T. S. Eliot Collection and Mr. Matthews's plans for a biography.

Before Mr. Eliot's death, we entered into an agreement whereby no one would have access to his letters without permission from Mr. Eliot or his heirs. Consequently, no one has had access to the letters without Mrs. Eliot's permission. This does not include his other manuscripts which have been made available to scholars in the regular way.

We regret the situation very much, but at the moment we feel we must honour Mrs. Eliot's position. Has Mr. Matthews discussed with Mrs. Eliot the possibility of having access to the letters without quoting them?

We shall be eager to help Mr. Matthews in any way we can. If he wishes to visit the Library in spite of the restriction on the use of the letters, he should address a letter to Mrs. Mary Hirth, Academic Centre

Librarian. It will be useful if she can know when to expect him and if she can have information about his proposed research for her files.

I am sorry not to be more encouraging. With kindest regards, Sincerely, F. W. Roberts, Director Humanities Research Centre.

So – that puts us back to square one again I think.

May 25, [1971]

A letter from JOHN FINLEY, dated May 22, former Master of ELIOT House, Harvard University.

Dear Tom: The present Master of Eliot House is Alan Heimerd. Tom Eliot's Collection has in fact long since gone to the Houghton Library. He himself decided on the change after his brother Henry's death, who had taken chief responsibility. The House, moreover, lacked the Houghton's means to acquire later items than those of the original Collection, which was started by Mrs. Eliot Senior and continued by Henry. Tom had hoped – what indeed would have been nice – that the House had funds for its library comparable to those of an English college. But, alas, there seems no possibility. . . . (and the rest of the letter is personal) Signed: Yours, John.

May 31, [1971]

Yesterday I had a talk with COLIN OLIVER who was down here with some of his family for the weekend, to ask his advice about what I should say to DU SAUTOY when I see him in his office on the 9th June; and he wasn't able to give me very much help. I think he agreed with me that the only thing I could do really – the best thing I could hope for – would be to make DU SAUTOY, in some way or other, feel rotten!

One thing I plan to do, which I didn't tell Colin about, is to hand DU SAUTOY a typed sheet of misprints that I have spotted in various Faber & Faber publications, which I am presumably just giving him out of the goodness of my heart. Colin agreed that I should keep, not as cool as possible, but very, very cool; and perhaps start off by asking DU SAUTOY what he knows about me. Does he know anything about me? Then somewhere along the way, get him to say whether or not I can expect permission to quote published material. The answer, I am sure, will be no; and eventually get him to answer the question, is he trying to prevent me from publishing this book? I have a shrewd suspicion that the upshot of this meeting may be to make me feel rotten instead of MR. DU SAUTOY!

Today, I believe, is the last day of my first year on this job, and perhaps I should try to cast up the accounts.

According to my contract with Harper & Row I have three years from 1st June, 1970 to do this book in. In the first year I have read all, or part, of about eighty books; of the items listed in GALLUP's biography I have read, or looked at, 216 items. I have collected twenty-three folders of notes; a correspondence file with several hundred letters; photocopies of many of ELIOT's letters; an illegal transcript of the BBC television programme (whose date I have forgotten) called The Mysterious MR. ELIOT; I have records of ELIOT reading The Four Quartets and Old Possum's Book of Practical Cats; and the rest of his poetry readings are on order.

I can say that I'm getting used to ELIOT's poems, though I can't honestly say I understand them. And what are the prospects? Well, (1) to write ELIOT's life, based on the scraps I can scavenge from the garbage pails in the area-ways, and to finish it no later than a year from now; to make sure that I'm not beaten to the draw by VALERIE and Fabers' change of mind, and their appointing an official biographer: (2) to write it without being allowed to quote one line of ELIOT's poetry or a phrase of his critical writing: or (3) to cut the losses [breaks off]

* * *

After one of the verses, <u>The Country Walk</u>, "an epistle to MISS E H with the humble compliment of her obliged servant, the author" MISS HALE has written this note: "Written, I think, the summer of '37 or '38 while visiting at Stamford House, Chipping Camden, Glouc., where TSE visited my uncles and aunt (Reverend and MRS. JOHN CARROLL PERKINS, D. D.) and where we often took long walks in the country about Gloucestershire." And the other set of verses called <u>Morgan Tries Again</u> is about one of his cats, Cat Morgan. EMILY HALE has written a note to his, a footnote to MISS SWAN, the devoted receptionist for many years at Faber & Faber, 24 Russell Square, London, "who welcomed me always on visits to the Publishing House."

ELLIE DU VIVIER, a cousin of EMILY HALE's, told me that EMILY HALE was in love with ELIOT and hoped to marry him. The fact that he wrote more than a thousand letters to her seems to bear this out.

May 19, [1971]

Letter from me to FRANCES LINDLEY.

> Dearest Frances: Interim report. Several balls in the air at the moment; if even one bounces instead of squishing, I'll be surprised. On the advice of an expert in copyright law I've now written to Bond (Houghton Library at Harvard) and Mrs. Hirth (Librarian at the University of Texas) asking them to state by what legal right they refuse me <u>access</u> to their ELIOT material (the right to quote anything is something else again; a later problem).
>
> The 'official' Eliot biography turned out to be a false alarm. Or rather, a prophecy rather than a report; the Oxford Press man who was misunderstood by my friend Fawcett (see my letter of April 24)

meant that Faber & Faber would soon be forced into commissioning such a biography – and he did say that already, on the strength of that probability, candidates for the job were queuing up. After Valerie had again refused to see me I wrote to Du Sautoy, not mentioning the rumour, asking <u>him</u> to see me, and he replied that he would, without the builders were still with them.

Du Sautoy seemed a cool but not unpleasant character, and the results of our interview, which lasted about forty minutes I should say, were about as I expected. It was not unpleasant. I started by giving him a typewritten sheet of misprints which I had found in some Faber & Faber books – mainly paperbacks – and particularly I called his attention to one which advertised on the back some Faber & Faber titles; one which attempted to advertise <u>Rosencrantz and Guildenstern</u>, but instead of <u>Guildenstern</u> it had <u>Goldenstein</u>! He received the list of misprints in the same fine spirit in which it was offered.

The first question I asked him was: "What do you know about me?" His answer was that he didn't know much, but he'd looked me up in <u>Who's Who</u>, and he said: "I know you were a friend of T. S. Eliot's." I said: "Well, that's not quite true; I'd known him for a long time, but I wouldn't say that we were friends."

The second question I asked was: "Are you going to give me permission to quote from Eliot's published works?" He started to say: "That's rather difficult to answer..." But I said: "There <u>is</u> an answer."

Oh yes, there is an answer. The answer is, you can quote as much as is considered 'fair dealing.' But if you ask permission to quote, we shall refuse."

Question: "Do you agree that there's a case for a biography?" (At this point I quoted him not only

Eliot's own remarks in the lecture he gave at the University of Minnesota which was published in To Criticise the Critic, but also Professor Richard Ellman's inaugural address at Oxford – a brilliant speech on biography by the biographer of Joyce – who had a little fun with his own side by reminding his audience of Oscar Wilde who said that all great men have disciples, and biographies are usually written by Judas.)

Anyway, Du Sautoy agreed that there was a case, and a very strong case for a biography, and I said: "When do you think you'll change your minds and commission one?" His answer was that he couldn't say when; but he then went on to talk of the letters which have now been scheduled for publication in November, I think he said; and also The Waste Land which apparently is coming out about the same time. And I gather from what he said that the indications are that they may be reconsidering the whole question of an official biography after the letters are published, but not before.

My next question was: "Would you try to prevent publication of my book?" His answer was: "Oh no, unless of course you go beyond the 'fair dealing' in the quantity of quotes."

And my last question was: "What would you do if you were in my place?" For the answer to that I ought to put down a row of question marks!

He said that he hadn't heard when the Sencourt biography would finally be published – that it was a very bad book – that Sencourt had been "old and ill and not up to it." He also agreed that the Levy book, Affectionately, T. S. Eliot, was an excruciatingly bad book, and harmful to Eliot's memory. I said it made him out a pompous twit, and Du Sautoy seemed to agree.

We parted friendly. As I say, I rather liked him. I asked him [breaks off]

*   *   *

June 2, 1971

This letter from the Librarian at Princeton University, dated May 24, 1971:

> Dear Mr. Matthews: After more delay than I care to contemplate, for which I hope that I may be forgiven, I enclose photocopies of the two poems by T. S. Eliot about which you enquired. They were presented to the Library by Miss Emily Hale, as you indicated, and the annotations on the typescripts are in her hand.
> I enclose also a rather disorderly but I think usable identification of T. S. Eliot letters in the Collections of the Princeton University Library. Not included in this listing (because they will not be available for use to you or to me) are more than one thousand[52] letters of Eliot to Miss Emily Hale, presented by Miss Hale and with the stipulation that they be sealed until fifty years after her death and that of Eliot, or until roughly January 1, 2020. I hope that we shall see you at the Princeton University Library when you are next in this country. Cordially yours, William S. Dix.
> I said, "Slip of the typewriter?" "Not at all."

---

52 In Dix's letter, he referenced "1,000" letters, leading Matthews to think he meant "100" and it might have been a typo.

June 7, [1971]

Today I had a note from SCHUYLER JACKSON, who died in 1968. I have the three-volume set of the J. M. DENT edition of Dante's Divine Comedy, with the Italian on one side and the English on the other; the same edition, I think, that T. S. ELIOT had, and from which he taught himself what Italian he knew. I suppose this set came from SCHUYLER. I wanted to see something about the translation. I took down the Paradiso; inside it I found on a piece of old wrapping paper a pencilled note in his unmistakable hand. It read as follows: "Better than Ulysses; better than Karamazov or The Idiot – but not so good as your being alive. Read it (some day) and weep. S." The pages of the book were uncut.

June 8, [1971]

A letter this morning from my new literary agent, DEBORAH OWEN, dated June 7.

> Dear Mr. Matthews: My famous leads seem to have fizzled. How are things progressing at your end?
> I plan to talk to Alan Maclean and would like to know what's up before seeing him.
> Would you entrust me with your precious books for a little while longer? Yours sincerely, Deborah Owen.

To which I replied:

> Dear Mrs. Owen: Thank you for your letter of June 7. I have been hoping to hear from you in spite of knowing you must be fiercely busy.
> I'm just carrying on as if all's well, which of course it ain't. Still stymied on the Bodleian papers, though the last faint hope has not been extinguished yet. Mr. Du Sautoy of Faber & Faber is

seeing me in his office tomorrow; I don't expect to get any change out of him, but can't help looking forward to the meeting.

I leave for the States July 9; back August 16. I don't suppose you'll have a spare moment before I go, but I would like to have another lunch (I'd let <u>you</u> talk this time!) and have you meet my wife. Perhaps you and your husband could come down here for a weekend?

By all means keep my books as long as you need to. Yours sincerely,

June 10, [1971]

Yesterday I had my meeting with PIERRE DU SAUTOY, the Chairman of Faber & Faber, in his office, 3 Queen's Square, at half past ten in the morning. The building, very up-to-date and new, is a great contrast to the old Faber & Faber offices on Russell Square. It looked as if they had just moved in; the hallways were cluttered with lumber and unfinished bookcases, and workmen all over the building. Du Sautoy's secretary told me they had moved in on the 1st March but to give my regards to MRS. ELIOT.

June 16, [1971]

The book I'm about to read, <u>Dear Miss Weaver</u>, a life of Harriet Shaw Weaver, has given me two thoughts, just reading the introductory acknowledgements: (1) the number of people I should have seen and haven't — the great distance I still have to go; and (2) the great gaps there will have to be in my list of acknowledgments, or should I say: "No thanks whatever are due to the following: and then list all the people who have refused to see me, ignored my letters, or denied me access to collections of papers, withheld permission to quote copyright material.

June 21, [1971]

ANNE and CHINK FOWLE, who were here for the weekend, turn out to have been next-door neighbours and fairly good friends of MAURICE HAIGH-WOOD; and Anne held out some hopes to me that she might try, if not actually to bring us together, to find out, if she could, from HAIGH-WOOD what the chances were of seeing his sister's papers at the Bodleian. Anyway, that's to be listed under the heading of "Faint Hopes".

> Dear Sir Compton: As our mutual friend Joyce Weiner may have told you, I have undertaken to write a biography of T. S. Eliot. Since he left a memorandum enjoining his literary executor neither to encourage nor <u>countenance</u> any biography of him, I am, as you may imagine, encountering certain difficulties.
>
> I can't help feeling that one of the main reasons Eliot opposed the writing of his life was his tragic first marriage – which seems to have been the grit in the oyster shell that became a pearl of great price. That much I think is clear. But so far I have been able to discover very little about his first wife, Vivienne, who was apparently a tempestuous, talented and haunted creature.
>
> In the first volume of Bertrand Russell's autobiography there are several of his letters to show his intimacy with the Eliots when they were first married: he 'loved Eliot like a son'. They all lived together in Russell's London flat; when Vivienne was ill and needed a holiday and Eliot could not leave London, Bertrand Russell went with her to Torquay, where Eliot replaced him a few days later. This event was followed apparently by a rapid cooling of their friendship (the intimate letters break off, and when the correspondence is renewed,

nearly twenty-five years later, it is 'as simple and faithless as a smile and shake of the hand').

What I surmise is that Russell seduced Vivienne and that Eliot either knew or suspected it. What I only surmise, Joyce tells me that you'd most probably know. If you do know and are willing to tell me <u>how</u> you know it, I should be most grateful.

Pam and I still remember with great pleasure our lunch with you and Lady Mackenzie in London, surrounded by our Siamese cats. Pam joins me in warmest regards to you both. Yours sincerely, ...

About ten days later, SIR COMPTON sent me a polite but completely noncommittal reply: he declined my gambit, showed circumspection, said he really knew nothing about it.

June 22, 1971

(In US) Got word from BARBIE STURTEVANT (MRS. THEODORE STURTEVANT) that she wanted to see me. I wondered if she were going to ask me not to write the book. But what was on her mind was something very different. She was afraid that VALERIE knew about the letter she (BARBIE) had written to me (dated June 30, 1970) telling me what she could remember about her cousin TOM ELIOT – which she had written in good faith, before she had heard that "the family" were not supposed to tell me anything. I told her I couldn't remember whether I had said anything to VALERIE about it, but would look at my letters to her as soon as I got back to England.

BARBIE felt that for some reason she was in VALERIE's bad books, and was very upset about it. Last winter, she said, an old spinster cousin, "YAHYAH," had died in Cambridge, and she had reported this in a letter to VALERIE. The postal strike in Britain shut down soon afterwards, which might account for her not hearing from VALERIE for a month or so, but could not explain the protracted silence which VALERIE had not yet broken.

"YAHYAH" had left her house (on Berkeley Court in Cambridge) and all its contents, which included photograph albums, letters and papers written by TSE in boyhood and youth, to Barbie and her brother HOLMES. BARBIE had given this material on loan to MR. BOND of the Houghton Library at Harvard, who wanted to put it with the rest of the TSE papers, but BARBIE was in two minds about that. She felt that VALERIE valued these juvenilia—because they pre-dated her? because they came from his American youth, which she could not share and with which she had little sympathy? — too lightly, if at all. BARBIE is going to talk to her brother about the disposition of these papers. She wants HOLMES and me to meet: she thinks we would get on well, and that he might be willing to talk to me about TSE, with whom, BARBIE says, he was very close, and with whom he had done a good deal of literary work. (HOLMES is a Sinologist, has just been in Tokyo for a year and a half, and may now return to Harvard.)

I asked BARBIE if she had known EMILY HALE. Indeed she had. Did she know that MISS HALE had left more than 1,000 letters to the Princeton University Library which TSE had written to her? She thought the number of 1,000 might be an exaggeration, but she knew about the letters: MISS HALE had thought of publishing some of them, but "the family" had exerted pressure on her not to—and she hadn't.

July 26, [1971]

From my sister's at Harwich Port: I telephoned EDMUND WILSON to ask if he could see me. I talked to his wife ELENA, and she said that he would be very glad to see me this afternoon, so I drove over. PAM said she wouldn't come with me because she thought that we would do better without her, and to give him her respects.

I had my usual difficulty finding his house. ELENA WILSON let me in and went to fetch him, leaving me in a sitting room. I was shocked at his appearance: he shuffled in, in a dressing gown, with his face quite chop-fallen and a bad color. He seemed glad to see me; he asked if my wife were with me and why she hadn't come: I said she had said she thought we would do better without her and that she sent her respects. ELENA got him a whisky and me an iced tea. The whisky seemed to revive him, but very soon he said reproachfully to ELENA, "You see! My speech is affected (a, it was): I cannot pronounce my words properly." She said soothingly that he enunciated very distinctly. (He didn't: quite often I lost the operative word in one of his sentences, or had to ask him to repeat a name.)

He was not the same old ruthless pursuer of a single conversational fish: often a sentence would be enough to finish a subject, and he was quite amenable to the shifts and changes of a rather gossipy conversation. He told me what he had just written (a book about his house, which had been his father's, in upstate N.Y.), a "juvenile," several other things— "if God spares me." He asked me about the book on ELIOT. Which I was then writing.

I said: "I think BERTRAND RUSSELL seduced VIVIEN, ELIOT's first wife," Wilson said vigorously: "Yes, yes. I always thought so."

> W: What did you think of Ode? [The poem that appears in Ara Vos Prec and was never afterwards reprinted.]
>
> I: Not much. I could see why he dropped it.
>
> W: Oh, it was quite good—but the subject was horrible.
>
> I: ???
>
> W: I always supposed it to be about his wedding night. And when asked why he had dropped it, he said 'An oversight'—obviously disingenuous.

When I arrived ELENA said "He has a present for you"—and I guessed what it was: the family photograph, taken in front of his house by a team from Holiday several years ago. The camera team were just arranging the group when I drove up, and Wilson called out to me to join them. When one of the crew asked him who I was, he said "My son." The picture was to have appeared (perhaps it did) with an article about WILSON. Last time I had been to see him he wanted to show it to me, but in spite of his vaunt that he could lay his hands instantly on any item in his library, thanks to his filing system, he was unable to find it. But this time he had it ready. I got him to sign it (which he did with complaints about the increasing difficulty of writing even his name) and ELENA, and his daughter HELEN, who came in later. WILSON said (of me in the photo): "You look rather like a benignant bishop."

WILSON said that he had had a bad fall, followed by at least two strokes, and was now able, to work only two or three hours a day.

I told him some of my difficulties with the ELIOT book, and he asked me what point I had reached. He advised me not to read too many books about ELIOT. He said he had always thought of ELIOT as a mid-Westerner— "rather like yourself"—and asked if I had read a book "by a New Zealander" about TSE and WALT WHITMAN. When I said that TSE had denied any kinship with WALT WHITMAN and thought little of him, WILSON corrected me: "He thought WHITMAN a good prose writer." Wilson had not heard of EMILY HALE.

Before telephoning MRS. WILSON I phoned CONRAD AIKEN and had an almost one-sided conversation with him. He was grumpily monosyllabic and almost inaudible, but I gathered that he did not want to talk about ELIOT, that he was not well, that he was willing to see me, but suggested that I write to him. His wife finally took over, and corroborated these impressions—he could not see me in the morning, but remembered me and wished me well; I said I would look forward to seeing him "next time around." When I asked WILSON if he ever saw AIKEN, he said "Not for a long time. He has denounced me publicly"— though he didn't make it clear what AIKEN had "denounced" him for.

July 29, [1971]

Telephoned MRS. PURVES (TED SPENCER's sister) at Wonalancet (we were at Francis Cleveland's, in Tamworth, for the night); she was in Europe.

<u>August 5, Cambridge, Mass.</u>: Went to Cambridge to see MRS. BENDER, the ex-wife of TED SPENCER, and had half an hour's conversation with her. It turns out that she was married to Ted only seven months before he died. His first wife, who apparently divorced him, is now living in Switzerland.

MRS. BENDER, pleasant-faced, rather pug-dog looking, academic wife type, said that she had known ELIOT only on a few occasions; that the correspondence between Ted and himself was always brief and cryptic, referring to dates of their next meetings, and that the talk about the technicalities of verse-writing was not very interesting to her. She said that he was not in Cambridge when Ted died, but had been there, teaching, the fall of the previous year; that he was very kind to her after TED died, and she saw him in London later. There didn't seem to be anything interesting that she said. When she heard I was going to Stockbridge she suggested that I stop and see MRS. ELLERY SEDGWICK, which I plan to do.

August 6, [1971]

PAM and I stopped at Archie MacLeish's house in Conway, Mass., for lunch, with MRS. MACLEISH and his son KENNETH who was a bearded Zeus or Henry Chopin-like type, now working for the National Geographic, and full of his travels. After lunch, when I was sitting with ARCHIE and his wife ADA, he asked me about the ELIOT job, and I recited for him. He had not heard of the veto and was quite sympathetic. He showed me a copy of Ara Vos Prec, the very rare edition with the misprint in the title—and we looked at Ode together, and by God, I think EDMUND WILSON was right; I think it is about his marriage night. I think he endured the boredom and the horror of married life, but never experienced the glory until flaccid old age, when it had become one of the gifts reserved for age.

August 7, [1971]

Stockbridge, Mass.: Went to see MRS. WILLIAM ELLERY SEDGWICK today, and found that she knew all the cast of characters, and was sympathetic. She hadn't heard of the veto, but couldn't add anything directly of her own knowledge. She did suggest, however, that I should get in touch with JACK SWEENEY in Ireland, ROBERT LOWELL in Oxford or London, I. A. RICHARDS, who is apparently moving to England for good, and HARRY LEVINE. She did add a caution that JACK SWEENEY, as a Catholic, might take the veto seriously; I don't know why, quite.

August 9, [1971]

Dinner with FRANCES LINDLEY, and much talk. She gave me the names of several people to see, and calmed my fears, or reassured me at least about the necessity of shortening my schedule on the ELIOT book. She seemed to be quite relaxed about that. She is very insistent, and I agree with her, I think—well, to put it negatively—that VALERIE is barking up all kinds of wrong trees when she overlooks or disregards or minimises ELIOT's American youth, American roots, American beginnings. We both agreed passionately that he is, was and will be an American poet, and that his end is to be found in his beginnings. Two of the people that she was anxious for me to see are WALKER EVANS whom I just missed in Boston, and DJUNA BARNES whose book, Night Wood, I think I reviewed when it first appeared but which I cannot remember anything about.

August 10, [1971]

I rang up DJUNA BARNES, who lives on Patchin Place, and asked if I could come down and see her about ELIOT. She'd heard about the veto, and said she never told anybody anything. FRANCES had told me that she had something like twenty-eight letters from ELIOT, but was down on Harpers, so not to mention Harpers. I didn't mention the letters even. I told her she wouldn't know who I was, but I think she had a suspicion, and when I told her I was writing a life of ELIOT she said, "Why should you? Why should anybody want to write anybody's biography? Put yourself in his position." I said, "Well, that I couldn't do because I could never imagine it." Anyway, she was very agreeable, quite firm, she wouldn't see me; and I was just as relieved as not, not to have to go down to Patchin Place on a day in the nineties in New York!

    I then did get hold of a WALKER EVANS, and he is to drive over to New Haven and meet me at the Beinecke Library where I am going tomorrow to see DONALD GALLUP, the bibliographer of ELIOT.

August 11, [1971]

Went to New Haven by an early train to see DR. GALLUP at the Beinecke Library. A steaming day but this time the train was air-conditioned. He seemed to me perhaps a little less sympathetic than he had the last time, but that may have been my imagination. He was receptive enough and he gave me about forty minutes of his valuable time. I asked him several questions; one was a thing that LOUIS KRONENBERGER had asked me—whether VIVIENNE had collected some of her own contributions to the <u>Criterion</u> and brought out a small book under her own name. GALLUP had never heard of it. Then I asked him about <u>Ode</u> which Wilson thinks was about his wedding night, which was never reprinted after its appearance in Ara Vos Prec. He seemed to think that the dates on the typescript which don't appear in the printed version (July 4, 1918, I think it was) sufficiently prove that it could not have been written about his wedding night. I don't agree.

One of the things I wanted to ask him was whether he thought ELIOT was a queer, but I failed to bring myself to do it. Perhaps because he's a little bit of a queer himself!

I told him about the Bodleian papers; he hadn't heard about them. He thinks that although the Bodleian can make what disposition of them they like as far as allowing people to see them, he thinks that VALERIE can't get them. But neither can I, of course. He says that ELIOT letters won't be out for years. The Waste Land is now due—I think he said—in November.

HELEN GARDNER, it appears, has been here lately; I wonder what those two are putting their heads together about. He had heard rumours about an official biography, but nothing definite. He thinks that when they do appoint a biographer, there will have to be not one, but two. Someone who appreciates the early ELIOT might not much like the later one.

GALLOP told me that ELIOT had said to him—I think to him, but anyway he said it of VIVIENNE—that she was the only woman he knew who had a mind like a man.

GALLUP says that I can get around the quotation difficulty by quoting as much as "fair dealing" will allow, and then paraphrasing a lot. He agrees that the candidates for the official biographer have probably been lining up for some time. He thinks that I can take my allotted time, however, as it will take the official biographer four or five years to do the job. Is GALLUP neutral, or is he a listening post? I wish I knew.

WALKER EVANS picked me up at the Library and took me to lunch at Moreys and then delivered me to the station. WALKER said, in Harper's Bazaar, he thinks, perhaps some time in the last ten years, there was an article about ELIOT and his mother which said that he was terrified of her, and went to England to get away from her. I must find that article if possible.

* * *

[page begins here] there was any notice of it in the press, and MRS. OAKELEY said that reporters kept coming to the door to make enquiries and were constantly being turned away

She thinks that HAYWARD minded ELIOT's leaving, and especially not being told; but she also thinks it was something of a relief to have him go. They were both ill a good deal and their illnesses seemed to alternate; and she thought that HAYWARD, particularly, felt the strain of it, and that with ELIOT gone there was less to look after. That was her impression, at least.

The French housekeeper, whom they called MADAME, stayed on about two years, MRS. OAKELEY said. Then HAYWARD got a man in, Askwith, to look after him. HAYWARD, when he died, left him quite a lot of money, and on the anniversary of HAYWARD's death, every year until he himself dies, Askwith ran a memorial in The Times, sometimes with rather dark sayings, or embarrassing sayings. One example she gave me: "All your prophecies have come true."

He also told MRS. OAKELEY that shortly after ELIOT's marriage he had seen ELIOT with his wife VALERIE in the park (presumably Hyde Park) and she was treating him like a baby— or she herself was acting like a nannie: "Come along, run, run, run!"

In the flat at Cheyne Walk they kept one cat, originally bought by HAYWARD to keep the French housekeeper happy, in the kitchen. It had the most expensive food, and apparently a great number of operations, also very expensive.

She said that ELIOT's bedroom was very spare and spartan, a crucifix above his single bed, one bookcase, filled mainly with theological books, and one chair, as far as she can remember. He had only a sixty watt bulb in his bedroom at about the time that money was rolling in from The Cocktail Party, and when HAYWARD said, "Don't you think we should do something about the Flat?" ELIOT said, "Well, perhaps I might have a better light in my room." She believes that the flat was re-decorated with the money.

HAYWARD never invited any member of his family when ELIOT was there, and his sister says that she had to make an appointment to meet him, HAYWARD, which isn't so unnatural as it might seem considering that the man was an invalid. She said HAYWARD and ELIOT had their meals separately.

She liked ELIOT very much but was rather afraid of him. She and her husband went with him once to a garden party at Buckingham Palace, which she regards as "the most wonderful afternoon of my life", and said he was the most charming, simple person you could imagine. They spent the whole afternoon together.

About The Cocktail Party, HAYWARD told his sister that he had, in a sense, written part of it because he had supplied some of the dialogue that people say at cocktail parties, ELIOT not being very familiar with that subject.

His sister said that in Bina Gardens, which was HAYWARD's first flat in London after he left Cambridge, they had a kind of club (she can't remember the name) in which all the members were called by pseudonyms. HAYWARD was known as "Tarantella" and ELIOT as "Possum". They published a privately circulated pamphlet which she said is now in the British Museum. (also at King's College: Noctes Binaniae)

Later the same day MOURA BUDBERG came for the weekend, and told me her own version of the parting between HAYWARD and ELIOT, and she is quite sure that her version is the correct one.

She was then translating and HAYWARD was editing Turgenev's On the Eve, and they used to meet once or twice a week. The day before ELIOT was married, HAYWARD rang MOURA and made a date to meet her two days later. The next day he rang her in the afternoon and without giving any reason said that they couldn't possibly meet then. Then he said, "I will meet you next week."

When MOURA arrived on the appointed day, HAYWARD was full of bitterness and malice, but very upset really. MOURA remembers how the flat smelled of loneliness.

HAYWARD then told her everything. That dreadful man, as he called him, had secretly taken away all his things, little by little, and left at 9 a.m. Then he telephoned about lunchtime to say that he had married VALERIE and that he was not coming back.

HAYWARD was so staggered that he had not a word to say, and hung up. What particularly angered him was, he said, "Think of the treacherousness of a man taking all his shirt and all his ties, little by little."

On the evidence of these two accounts it would appear that ELIOT had not had the nerve to face HAYWARD with the news himself, as had happened in CHRISTOPHER SYKES's version. It will be interesting now to see what CHRISTOPHER SYKES says about this.

August 23, [1971]

I met ROBERT LOWELL only once; it was some time during the war – 1940 something. He was then married to JEAN STAFFORD, and I believe had just finished a year in a labour camp to which he was sent because of being a conscientious objector. There was some fear that he could be sent back for another year unless he was given some sort of a cover, and he and his wife came to see me about this. We were living at 876 Park Avenue at the time.

JEAN STAFFORD, I remember, was absolutely sloshed with Martinis and I foolishly gave her another. As I remember it, Lowell only sat on the sofa looking miserable and was completely silent the whole time. She wanted me to put him, theoretically, on the staff of TIME, which she thought would protect him, and of course I agreed to do this. That's the only dealings I've ever had with him.

I wrote the following letter today: "August 23, 1971. ROBERT LOWELL, Esq., 80 Redcliffe Square, London, S.W.10.

Dear Mr. Lowell: Harper & Row have commissioned me to write a life of T. S. Eliot. As you do doubt know, MR. ELIOT left a memorandum with his Will forbidding his literary executor to "facilitate or countenance" any biography of him – a veto which will effectively postpone the inevitable official life until all who knew him at first hand are dead.

In the short run, and as a family matter, this may be regarded as a good thing for Mr. Eliot (only the enquiring worm will have tried his well-preserved complacency); in the long run, and as a matter that concerns all of us, I think it a moot question, at the very least. The next generation, or the one after that, may find this posthumous shyness impossible to defend, impossible not to speculate about.

In any case, my studies for the book are going ahead, although you can easily imagine some of the obstacles and difficulties. It may be that you agree with Mr. Eliot (the later Eliot, that is: in 1956 he had written, "I do not suggest that the personality and the private life of a dead poet constitute sacred ground on which the psychologist must not tread...nor is there any reason why the biographies of poets should not be written"). Our mutual friend Robert Fitzgerald wants me to drop the whole thing – I am hoping, however, that you may be on my side of the question – or that, even if you are not, you will be willing to see me and talk about it. I get to London infrequently, but would be very glad to meet you for lunch either at the Athenaeum or the Garrick, if you will name a day that is convenient for you. Yours sincerely,

ROBERT LOWELL, MILGATE PARK, BEARSTEAD, MAIDSTONE, KENT. September 2, 1971.

Dear Mr. Matthews: I'd be glad to talk to you, but I can be of no help. I suppose anyone must have the right to try to keep back a biography. Robert Bridges even seems to have succeeded – maybe there was little event to tell. I am sure what Eliot wanted to veil was his tortured first marriage. Why not? But will it work?

I've just been through something similar. An author can almost make more money on his papers: first, last drafts, letters from friends etcetera. I'd just as soon throw my whole business into the fire, not really because of personal disclosures, but simply because most of us do posterity a favour by leaving as little as possible behind – those reams of paper, enough to use up every tree in Maine and Oregon! Still, for me money must decide. Little harm, little good.

Eliot in his last post-war years was a close and dear friend. I don't feel the same way as he about his biography. I am sure I would read one of him. Yet it was a reasonable wish, perhaps correct. Frost hasn't gained by his, though in the end it won't perhaps matter. Many things, often not to Frost's credit, are important. Most of the long books should have been junked. And I like good personal details more than textual criticisms. I can't go against Eliot's wishes and help you. And of Valerie's, also my friend. I'm sure you know her stubbornness. You have a very rough road. Maybe Robert is right. Yours sincerely, Robert Lowell.

P.S. Excuse this windy letter. In the back of my mind somewhere is our pleasant meeting thirty years ago.

August 27, [1971]

MRS. ROLAND OAKELEY, sister of JOHN HAYWARD and a friend of ELAINE BINNEY, came to lunch today with ELAINE, and talked at some length about her brother JOHN. She assured me that she had the only correct version of the parting between ELIOT and HAYWARD.

ELIOT went on holiday just before he got married (this is her version) and as he left he said "Adieu" to the French housekeeper, who noted it and wondered why he hadn't said "Au revoir".

He telephoned the news of his marriage to HAYWARD the day afterwards. HAYWARD the put it about that "Tom has eloped with his secretary."

When HAYWARD spoke to ELIOT on the telephone he said: "I'm delighted to hear it but why didn't you tell me?"

ELIOT said: "Because I thought you'd be so cross."

This was told by HAYWARD to his sister, MRS. OAKELEY, at a children's party at his flat the day on, or after, ELIOT's marriage, before [breaks off]

(Here something went wrong with the recorder, but I think the only thing that was lost was a reply from VALERIE ELIOT dated 30th September.

> Dear Mr. Matthews: Thank you very much for your letter. I appreciate your courtesy in writing, and am happy to know that you had no part in this matter. Yours sincerely, Valerie Eliot.

Very stately. And her signature is really something to see now. It's 'Val' – then a great Valkyrie swoop – then 'erie'. When I showed it to Pam she said, "My, she's getting like Napoleon, isn't she!"

September 22: [1971] This letter has just arrived from Wolfson College, Oxford.

> September 20, 1971. Dear Mr. Matthews: Thank you for your letter of 8th September. I feel sure that my time is not more precious than yours, but in any case I should be delighted to see you again. I have no notion about the rules of the Bodleian—I expect they have powers to make any rules they please, provided they do not contravene specific conditions laid down either by donors, or by the University, or by the Government. The only person worth speaking to on this subject is, I suspect, the Librarian himself, a perfectly reasonable man called Shackleton to whom I should be glad to introduce you. If you are coming to Oxford in any case, would you like me to try and make a date with him for you, and come to see me before or after? As for days, would you like to come and have lunch with me—it's a very rough and ready meal here—on 13 or 14 or 15 October? Yours sincerely, Isaiah Berlin.

September 23, [1971]

> A number of bits and pieces from Frances Lindley. Among them a letter to her from Thomas Lipscomb, Editor-in-Chief of Dodd, Mead & Co. who are just about to produce the Sencourt biography. His letter to her dated 9th September, says, in part: "...This is the letter I am sending out to reviewers, to try and put the genre they're dealing with in Sencourt's <u>Memoir</u> squarely in front of them. I don't think that the average, or even above average, reviewer is literate enough to tell the difference between a memoir, a biography, and a Kiwanis Memorial Lecture, and is likely to review any one of the three as the other, complaining that it's not the third. No doubt my letter will confuse them all

the more, in which case the lazy ones will paraphrase passages from it (I hope). Then they'll be only 75% off their mark, instead of the usual 99%.

Nothing would please me more than that favorable reception of the Memoir would relax the sphincters of the Eliot estate through a reasonable state of controlled hysteria. So I hope Publishers' Weekly and other important reviewers will call you and get more information on the Matthews biography. If this should scare up some interest (even though no one in publishing ever follows up on obvious leads) I only hope that you will make clear to them the time differential between the appearance of my little Memoir and Matthews's full-scale biography, so the poor dears won't be sitting on their hands waiting for the Matthews biography which is two years away. (Signature).

Here is the relevant paragraph of the letter that he is sending out to reviewers:

Sencourt's Memoir is not a literary masterpiece, nor does it answer many of the questions which will probably have to await a biographer who succeeds in gaining access to Eliot's papers some years from now. Mr. T. S. Matthews, who is perhaps ideally suited for the task, is currently writing a biography of Eliot which is scheduled for publication in the spring of 1973 by Harper & Row. And yet, as his editor Mrs. Frances Lindley informs me, Mr. Matthews is meeting the same senseless blockade by the Eliot Estate others have encountered. We can only hope that Mrs. Eliot and the Estate will recognize their opportunity to co-operate with a first-rate biographer like Matthews, rather than choose to enlist the first of what would undoubtedly be a long, dreary line of official biographers, from whose pedantic leavings we would be forced to try to piece together the life of the ironic, melancholy, and all too human subject whom they could not possibly understand.

Well, blow me down!
FRANCES, in her recent letters, seems quite excited about the papers in the BERTRAND RUSSELL archives at McMaster University, and seems to be under the impression that anybody can walk in and simply cope them, and offers to send somebody if I can't find somebody myself. I only wish that what she thinks were true.

I forgot to say that several days ago someone from the <u>Life</u> office in London telephoned me and said that Dave Sherman in New York wanted me to review the SENCOURT biography. I just told them to tell DAVE SHERMAN that I wouldn't do it for a million dollars. "A million dollars?" they said. "Two million!"

September 25, [1971]

CHRISTOPHER SYKES, who is spending the weekend here, has just read over the typed notes on our dinner conversation some months ago in London and has been kind enough to write me the following corrected page. This is Sykes speaking: (see page &&& where this is typed in context.)

CHRISTOPHER SYKES, to whom I showed the copy of the Lipscomb letter, was very strongly of the opinion that I would do well to write to MRS. VALERIE ELIOT and dissociate myself from MR. Lipscomb. He pointed out that somebody was bound to bring the letter to her attention. So I have just written her the following letter:

Dear Mrs. Eliot: Harper & Row have just sent me a copy of a letter written by Mr. Thomas H. Lipscomb, Editor-in-Chief of Dodd, Mead & Co., which he has sent out to reviewers of Robert Sencourt's Memoir of T. S. Eliot. The following paragraphs in the letter concerns me (and I quote the paragraph).

[TSM has crossed out first paragraph] "'~~Sencourt's Memoir is not a literary masterpiece, nor does it answer many of the questions which will probably have to await a biographer who succeeds in gaining access to Eliot's papers some years from now. MR. T. S. Matthews, who is perhaps ideally suite for the task, is currently writing a biography of Eliot which is scheduled for publication in the spring of 1973 by Harper & Row. And yet, as his editor Mrs. Frances Lindley informs me, Mr. Matthews is meeting the same senseless blockade by the Eliot Estate others have encountered. We can only hope that Mrs. Eliot and the Estate will recognize their opportunity to co-operate with a first-rate biographer like Matthews, rather than choose to enlist the first of what would undoubtedly be a long, dreary line of official biographers, from whose pedantic leavings we would be forced to try to piece together the life of the ironic, melancholy, and all too human subject whom they could not possibly understand.~~'"

I neither know Mr. Lipscomb nor have had any dealings whatever with him, and I resent and reject what he says here. I am bringing this matter to your attention because I feel sure that someone else will if I don't; and I should not like you to think me capable of this sort of behaviour. Yours sincerely,

I also have sent a copy of my letter to MRS. ELIOT to Frances Lindley, with no comment.

CHRISTOPHER SYKES suggests that I get hold of NOEL BLAKISTON, who has retired from the Record Office, lives at 6 Markham Square, S.W.3., and says that he knew HAYWARD very well, but ELIOT not at all. SYKES also told me of a woman named HILDA TREVELYAN – he thinks a MISS HILDA TREVELYAN – and doesn't know exactly how she fits into the TREVELYAN family, who was, according to him, in love with ELIOT, hoped to marry him, and turned against him very bitterly when he married VALERIE, and as SYKES expresses it, "hotted up" HAYWARD after their parting. She was extremely bitter against ELIOT.

This is another lady that I've never heard of, to add to the ELIOT list.

September 30, [1971]

A letter from FRANCES LINDLEY dated September 27: "Just talked with our man in Toronto, whose 007 blood is all a-tingle at the prospect of smuggling a 'student' into the RUSSELL archives to copy the five pertinent letters in longhand. He'll let me know."

October 1, [1971]

When CHRISTOPHER SYKES was here for the weekend lately, he mentioned a MISS HILDA TREVELYAN as being a lady who had been much disappointed by ELIOT's marriage to VALERIE. This morning I got a letter from him:

> Last night I met Humphrey Trevelyan who is now Lord Trevelyan. I got the name wrong of TSE's friend. She is Miss Mary Trevelyan, and Humphrey's sister, and she felt very much betrayed when TSE went off with Valerie. I told Humphrey about your researches and book and he is going to tell his sister about it, and suggested that you write to her. He said she is in the telephone book but feel dubious about M. H. Trevelyan, 60 Fawnbrook Avenue, S.E.24.! It might be as well to check on the phone: 274 2674. Humphrey's Address is 13 Wilson Street, S.W.1.

October 7, [1971]

I'm sending this letter this morning to JOHN SPARROW, the WARDEN of All Souls', All Souls' College, Oxford.

> Dear Warden: I know you are not an admirer of T. S. Eliot, but I believe you are on the side of common sense and fair play. Also I gather you are not averse to an occasionally dust-up if the casus belli seems to warrant it. Therefore, although almost a stranger to you, I am applying to you for help.
>
> I have accepted a commission from Harper & Row, the New York publishers, to write a life of T. S. Eliot. As you probably know, he did not want his life written, and left a memorandum attached to his Will enjoining his literary executor (his widow) neither to "facilitate nor countenance" any biography of him. Although she herself admits that his injunction can only delay but not prevent the biography that must eventually be written, she is carrying out her task with a vim and vigour that seem above and beyond the call of duty.
>
> Eliot's first wife, Vivienne, from whom he parted in 1932 and who died in a mental hospital in 1947, left a Will dated March 5, 1936 in which the following paragraph appears:
>
> 'V. I give to the Bodleian Library Oxford absolutely and free of duty all my papers manuscripts diaries journals photographs albums and sketches except securities and books of account on condition that the said Library shall not permit any of the same to be altered erased added to quoted from or used for the purposes of any work of fiction.'
>
> When I learned of this bequest I applied to the Bodleian, as a senior member of the University and a serious student, asking to see these papers. I was told (a) that no one could see them ('until everyone is

dead'), (b) that they're not worth seeing, (c) that very few people know of their existence but that if there should be a 'hue and cry' the Bodleian will probably turn the papers over to the present Mrs. Eliot. When I asked by what authority these things were done, I was told: 'Oh, we make our own rules.'

Although I am no lawyer, it seems to me that the terms of Vivienne's Will do not preclude my right to see these papers and to make my own judgment of whether or not they are of value to a biographer of T. S. Eliot; and that the Bodleian is exceeding its authority (in the light of the terms of this bequest) in denying me access to the papers.

I write to ask you whether you find any justice in my case, and, if you do, whether you are willing to help me to get access to these papers. I expect to be in Oxford on November 24; but if you would like to discuss this matter further I could come to Oxford on any day that is mutually convenient, or if you prefer, meet you in London. Yours sincerely,

October 7, [1971]

(contd.): This morning I got a long-awaited letter from KENNETH BLACKWELL, the archivist of the BERTRAND RUSSELL archives at McMaster University:

October 4; Dr. Matthews: In reply to your letter of August 20th, I do not wish to bring a law suit on the University by sending out copies of Vivienne Eliot's letters without the required permission of the copyright holders, if they can be located. You well know the current Mrs. Eliot's attitude to the copyrights in her control. However, I will do what I regard as the researcher's job and write to her myself to ask who owns the copyright in Vivienne's letters.

I was wrong about my source having any additional information about Vivienne and Russell. She wrote me: 'I fear I could not, now, write anything worth having about Mrs. Eliot, whom I never met.' Yours sincerely, Kenneth Blackwell Archivist.

The same mail brought me a note from Frances, also dated October 4 enclosing a letter from Fitzhenry & Whiteside in Ontario. The note from Frances says:

Dearest Tom: I hope this makes you laugh. Fitzhenry the man in Toronto who is sending an agent to copy the letters in the Russell collection. Stefan Lorant is a Hungarian master of deceit (tautology?) who has swindled many publishers out of many dollars. All love, Frances.

Enclosed with her note is this letter to her from some character who signed himself "Sam Slick":

Chère Amie: We have assigned our agent A-101 to the mission. Elle s'habite à Hamilton. Elle a large soft brown eyes and a mind like Stefan Lorant. We anticipate results.
    However, we assure you, we are prepared to activate plan B, if
    At last, dear Diary, I can tell you a small piece of good news.

* * *

[new page] necessary. The quick brown fox jumped nimbly into the waiting bush as the rains came from the east. In confidence, Sam Slick.
    I then sent a cable to Frances, reading as follows:
    Toronto had better hurry. Blackwell alerting Valerie. (signed) Tom.

October 11, [1971]

PAM saw the following item in The Sunday Telegraph:

> John Sparrow, Warden of All Souls', will not be in residence at Oxford this term. He has taken sabbatical leave until the new year.
>   He is spending it writing in Italy. Like most chaste stylists, he composes slowly. But if what he brings from Venezia is as illuminating as his Mark Pattison and the Idea of a University, it will have been well worth waiting for.
>   All Souls' meanwhile has an acting Warden – Sir Humphrey Waldock, the international lawyer. I have not yet heard from Sir Humphrey.

October 12, [1971]

A letter today from MARY TREVELYAN.

> Dear Mr. Matthews: Your letter of October 5th has just come in. I am so sorry I shall not be in London on the dates you suggest coming to see me, as I leave for Northumberland today. I shall not be back in London again until the end of the month. Perhaps you would get in touch with me again later. However, although Tom Eliot and I were friend for the best part of twenty years, I doubt if I can give you much information which would be of real value to a biographer. But I would, of course, be interested to hear what you are doing. Yours sincerely, Mary Trevelyan.

    To which I replied, asking her if she could see me on the 23rd November, which is the next date on which I expect to be in London.
    Yesterday I wrote the following letter: "The Acting WARDEN, All Souls' College, Oxford.

Dear Sir: Some weeks ago I sent a letter addressed to the Warden of All Souls' that was intended for Mr. John Sparrow. Several days after I sent the letter I learned that he had gone on sabbatical leave and that you (whose name I am sorry to say escapes me) were taking his place. May I ask whether you forward my letter to Mr. Sparrow? And would you be kind enough to give me his address? Yours sincerely.

This morning I got the following letter dated November 4:

The Warden's Lodgings, All Souls' College.

Dear Mr. Matthews: I am sorry to have delayed in answering your letter of 7 October but I am taking a term off in Italy and put off replying until I could be in Oxford. I have come over for three or four days for the All Souls' celebrations and am taking the opportunity of dictating answers to letters that reached me recently in Venice, to which I return tomorrow and where I hope to stay until Christmas. I am afraid that my absence in Italy has removed me from the councils of the Bodleian, and will prevent me from attending meetings of the Curators and other committees for the rest of the year. As a result of this, I have no knowledge – apart from what you told me in your letter – of the circumstances in which the Bodleian has refused your request to look at the first Mrs. Eliot's papers; nor am I in a position to do anything about it, at any rate at present. "If you would like, I will look into the matter when I get back.

FRANCES also writes me about a Greek lady who's the widow of a close friend of ELIOT's, and her late husband wrote an article about it which she is apparently going to send me. I look forward to getting it.

FRANCES also sent me a review of the SENCOURT book by HUGH KENNER, the author of *The Invisible Poet, T. S. ELIOT*, and he gives the book very poor marks, but says that SENCOURT was the first to tell the story of ELIOT's writing from America to his wife, through a solicitor, that he had ordered a Deed of Separation to be drawn up, and asked if he could not find some less cruel way of telling her, said: "What other way can I find?"

KENNER says, in being the first to tell us that story, MR. SENCOURT hasn't told us what we'd need to know to judge ELIOT's ?? which is one reason why this memoir is ultimately so distasteful.

October 13, [1971]

The good news was in a letter from FRANCES LINDLEY dated October 8, with a footnote dated October 11. Here is part of it:

> ...Lipscomb of Dodd, Mead reported on the phone yesterday that he had received a letter from Valerie Eliot pointing out twenty errors of fact in the Sencourt and asking that the book be held up until they could be corrected. The book has, of course, already been shipped, but those errors – alleged errors – about which she seems to be right (80% he says) will be corrected in any second printing.
>
> He has already incorporated corrections received from Conrad Aiken and Samuel Eliot Morrison. Aiken, whose memoir of TSE I assume you have read, is also reputed to be the custodian of most of the poet's 'dirty poems'. Anyway I'll ask Lipscomb if we might have a copy of Valerie's corrections.

> The relevant Russell letters have been copied by the young lady and ought to have been in my hands by now.

Then the footnote:

> No mail today so I am not holding this up after all. I am waiting to receive them before sending this message on. The young lady was obliged to sign an affidavit saying she was not planning to publish them; if it turns out that you do want to, it would mean getting permission from Vivienne Eliot's Estate, I suppose. One startling phrase our Toronto man remembered out of Vivienne's letter to Russell: "Don't worry. Tom says the baby will have pointed ears.' Presumably TSE had pointed ears? Anybody know what became of that baby?

Well, I seem to remember something about pointed ears from MR. APOLLINAX. I thought perhaps it was a reference to him as a faun but I looked it up and on line sixteen it says: "I heard the beat of centaur's hoofs over the hard turf/As his dry and passionate talk devoured the afternoon./'He is a charming man' – 'But after all what did he mean?' – / 'His pointed ears...'"

FRANCES also sent me a copy of JOHN BARKHAM's review of the SENCOURT book for The Saturday Review, with a covering note from Barkham, saying:

> Here is my forthcoming review of the book on T. S. Eliot published by Dodd, Mead. In it I make reference to an Eliot biography by T. S. Matthews, to be published by Harper, 1973...I think Tom Matthews may want to see the anecdote I tell very briefly in the closing paragraphs.

And the relevant parts of Barkham's review is that

> ...in London T. S. Matthews, like Eliot himself an Anglo-American, is engaged on an Eliot biography due for publication in 1973...The poet's ban on the use of his papers published and unpublished applied equally to an old friend like Sencourt. Eliot's widow, whom he married late in life, is making no exceptions, as T. S. Matthews has doubtless discovered by now...I hope Matthews has more success than Sencourt in humanising the austere presence who was T. S. Eliot. Here, for example, is one incident in his life which occurred after World War II and which to the best of my knowledge has never been printed. It was told to me shortly before her death by the noted South African novelist and biographer Sarah Gertrude Millin, whose books were published by Eliot's firm of Faber & Faber.
>
> Eliot came to South Africa to spend a summer vacation in Mrs. Millin's seaside home near Cape Town. Late on the first night in reading through a volume of Eliot's collected verse, she came across the poem Burbank with a Baedeker with the following lines on Venice: 'The rats are underneath the piles. /The jew is underneath the lot.' Thought he hour was late, Mrs. Millin – her Jewish ire aroused – rapped on the door of Eliot's bedroom and demanded to know whether he had indeed written thus of Jews. When Eliot replied in the affirmative Mrs. Millin ordered him to leave her house in the morning, which he duly did.

October 16, [1971]

Well, dear Diary, the purloined letters have arrived, and of course they are a sad disappointment. They came with a covering letter from FRANCES LINDLEY's Canadian friend who was instrumental in getting them, saying:

> I enclose the five Bertrand Russell letters which it turns out we have not quite been able to hist from McMaster University inasmuch as our operator was required to sign a statement that the letters could not be published without permission of the copyright holders. So, while we have the letters, we have a rather heavy mortgage on them.
> I join you in hoping that your man will be able to obtain permission from Mrs. Eliot's Estate.

There are not five BERTRAND RUSSELL letters. There are three from VIVIENNE; the first one dated November 1, 1921, the other two not dated, but with a different address which I supposed, if we can trace, we may be able to find the date. The second one is from Crawford Mansions, W.1., the third from 57 Chester Terrace, S.W.1.

Then the other two letters, which are very brief; one of June 13, 1949, from BERTRAND RUSSELL to ELIOT, obviously thanking him for a note of congratulation on RUSSELL's getting the Order of Merit; and the last one, 23 May, 1964, also from RUSSELL to ELIOT, a three-line note thanking him for his note congratulating him on a broadcast.

The 'baby with the pointed ears' turns out to be, pretty certainly, RUSSELL's own legitimate son. The relevant paragraphs from VIVIENNE's letter of November 1, 1921, reads: "We both send very many congratulations and Tom says he is quite sure the baby <u>will</u> have pointed ears, so you need not be anxious. Even if not pointed at birth, they will sharpen in time."

October 19, [1971]

Went to London, called on NOEL BLAKISTON, who had been recommended to me by CHRISTOPHER SYKES (!) recently retired from the Record Office, at his house at 6 Markham Square. He was at Magdalene, Cambridge, when HAYWARD was at King's, and got to know him then, and they were good friends the rest of his life.

His story about the parting of HAYWARD and ELIOT was that ELIOT gave HAYWARD a letter, and HAYWARD read it, then said to ELIOT, who was hovering, "Sit down my dear Tom, and let's talk about it."

ELIOT said, oh no, no, he couldn't, the taxi was waiting.

BLAKISTON once saw ELIOT's room, although he didn't know ELIOT at all well. He said it was a monk's cell, where he slept, worked, and ate meals from a tray on his knew. The window looked out on a blank wall.

BLAKISTON thought HAYWARD was very brave about his illness; also bawdy, domineering at a dinner table, a conversationalist who tended to a monologue. He had beautiful small handwriting; BLAKISTON said he almost envied him, would like to have had his head, at least, but not the rest of his body.

The friendship between Blakiston and HAYWARD rather fell off after ELIOT left him, and eventually petered out, but he said he used to push HAYWARD's chair; never, apparently, coincidentally with ELIOT.

BLAKISTON thought HAYWARD dominated TSE, or thought he did.

I had lunch with DEBORAH OWEN, my literary agent, and she told me that she knew a young fellow named TIMOTHY WILSON who is the son-in-law of ANNE RIDLER, one of ELIOT's ex-secretaries. She said that WILSON was doing an interview with VALERIE, and also writing a piece for The Guardian on the facsimile edition of The Waste Land.

She said that WILSON was expecting to see me, so I rang him up and made a date to have a drink with him that afternoon. I found eh was very young, likeable, a free-lance journalist. ANNE RIDLER's husband, I believe, is printed to the Oxford Press, or has some connection with it.

Wilson's piece for The Guardian on The Waste Land will appear on November 8 when the book comes out, and he is to interview VALERIE a few days before that. He advised me, in effect, not to see his mother-in-law, but said that he would speak to her about me.

He didn't tell me all he knew, nor I him; we were wary of each other, but I think we got along all right.

Later that same day, I rang up PAM who reported that MUNBY had tried to get me by telephone, and had later come to the house, and she had given him a drink.

He said that my letter to VALERIE had made a deep impression on her, and seems to think that her mind may be changing; at any rate it may be a good idea for me to meet her lawyer who has great influence on her. Apparently, he will put me in touch with this gent.

Can it be that a bright interval approaches?

October 22, [1971]

The British edition of the SENCOURT book has just reached me, and although I've only given it a cursory look over, I would say that it is dull, badly written, but still makes my heart sink a bit. It may have cut the ground out from under me on several counts. One of them is the photographs; he's got one of the right Dry Salvages, and the origins of all the Four Quartets, and some ELIOT pictures I had never seen before, and one of VIVIENNE that I had never seen.

Now I must read it.

October 27, 1971 Lindley to TSM

... I have just had a long and very interesting lunch with young LIPSCOMB, SENCOURT's American editor. He is the last to make exaggerated claims for the book· nevertheless, he feels that, it casts some light on ELIOT and breaks the conspiracy of silence. He showed me VALERIE's list of 88 errors of fact.

I read it; one or two seemed useful (for The Bird Song of San
Sebastian, read The Love Song of SS); most are trivial and
imprecise: she says there were no children at Burnt Norton
when ELIOT went there. How does she know?

LIPSCOMB would not give me a copy of the list, because
he is waiting to see VALERIE's next move. In the letter to
him accompanying her list (she calls it a Schedule) she
threatened make the list public if he did not hold up the
edition to incorporate her corrections. He will not make
it public unless she acts on this threat. I am sure, however,
that he will give us the two or three valid changes such as
the title above.

More particularly be told me of lunching in London last
week with NIGEL TILSON (?) who does the "Insight" column in
the Sunday Times... or is it the London Times on Sunday? He
told MR. INSIGHT that he feels VALERIE is anxious to suppress
"the dark lady" and – my extrapolation – all the darkness
in ELIOT. Supposedly a column on the subject will appear on
Sunday, October 31, and this may well provoke some action on
VALERIE's part.

Having read VALERIE's letter and her Schedule I am
arrogant, enough to believe that I suddenly "see" her.
She seems to have that rigid middle-class English mind
which excludes all that it cannot easily comprehend.
Incidentally, a schoolmate or VALERIE's declares that at
age 15 she had already determined to marry a famous writer,
and that she planned to accomplish this by first becoming
his secretary.

Your copy of The Waste Land has not yet arrived, but we
will send it along to you the minute it comes in. I judge you
will have to work out which are VIVIENNE's corrections and
which are Ezra Pound's....

October 23, [1971]

A long delayed answer from I. A. RICHARDS.

From Cambridge, Mass., 19th October. Dear Mr. Matthews: Our delay in returning to England has been by accident and it is still not clear just when we will be back; probably before June.

    On the book: I know about the impediments. To be frank I do not see why T. S. Eliot's clearly expressed wishes should not be respected. See the Kipling verses he prefixed to his selection from Kipling's verse.

    I find myself entirely of the same view. So I do not see how I could be of much help. Though I would gladly talk of it all with you when we get back. Sincerely, I. A. Richards.

    P.S. I have gone, you know, often on record as being against biographical doings about poets. Yours sincerely, (no signature).

November 8, [1971]

Last night VALERIE made an hour's broadcast on BBC Radio 3 in celebration of the publication of the facsimile edition of <u>The Waste Land</u>, and I hope I got most of it on tape; I know that they wouldn't give me a transcript of it.

    The following morning I got the very handsome edition sent to me by FRANCES, costing twenty-two and a half dollars; I've just glanced at it so far but I've also seen a very lengthy review in the <u>New York Book Review</u> by a woman named HELEN VENDLER. It's a very competent job and shows, I think, what effect this book is going to have on ELIOT's reputation. I think that, quite unwittingly and certainly against her intention, she has done her husband a great disservice, and one; he would have greatly resented.

    In <u>The Man from New York</u>, a biography of JOHN QUINN, page 540, it tells about ELIOT's having sent this original of <u>The Waste Land</u> to QUINN, for which incidentally he paid ELIOT $140, and which his niece, after his death, sold to the

Berg Collection for $18,000 without saying anything to ELIOT about it, ELIOT wrote to QUINN:

> You will find a great many sets of verse which have never been printed and which I sure you will agree never ought to be printed and in putting them in your hands I beg you fervently to keep them to yourself and see that they never are printed.

And this is completely disregarded by VALERIE and I think it has irreparably damaged the accepted image of her adored husband.

HELEN GARDNER also says it is impossible to praise too highly the work of the printer, VIVIEN RIDLER, who is ANN RIDLER's husband and printer for the Oxford Press, I believe. But my copy distinctly says, "Printed in the United States of America"

Could it be possible that the book was printed twice? I was so curious about it I rang up MUNBY again, and he says no, no, that couldn't be possible, and I think he said he had compared my list of mistakes with his copy and they were there right enough.

I suppose this means that either RIDLER had nothing to do with the British edition – then why should his name appear? – or that HELEN GARDNER hasn't spotted any of these mistakes.

And then when I said, "Why was there such a clandestine wedding?", he seemed to take it for granted that that was because he had compromised her. I said that RUSSELL seemed to think that she was a vulgar little thing. He said, oh no, he didn't think so. No, not vulgar.

But he was very cool about ELIOT. He said that ELIOT used to give him good advice or a kind of pep talk about his writing, saying he must work harder; and then when Faber began to publish his books (Sacheverell Sitwell's) that ELIOT took absolutely no interest, gave him no help, which he apparently didn't particularly like.

He thought there was only one poet possible for a generation and that was Yeats; that ELIOT's finest poem was The Waste Land, and that after that there was a great falling-off, that his later poems and the Quartets were awfully dry.

I got an anecdote out of Georgia, Lady Sitwell. She said this happened in 1927, which sounds a bit early, but she was apparently being introduced to her new sister-in-law, EDITH, and her mother was along. She knew that EDITH didn't smoke so she brought her own cigarettes. VIVIEN was there too and when Georgia offered her mother a cigarette, VIVIEN said in a horror-struck tone, "You wouldn't take one from her!" – the strong implication being that in 1927 she was already so unbalanced that she had these tremendously suspicious feelings about people.

November 12, [1971]

I've been looking through the Facsimile of The Waste Land, a copy of which FRANCES sent to me, a so-called beautiful job of book production, at a most tremendous price, twenty-two dollars and a half; the American edition. The book itself, and VALERIE ELIOT's part in it, have been getting a very good Press – everyone has been saying what a beautiful job of editing she did – and it was consequently with somewhat of a shock that I began to notice bits of careless proof-reading, and worse; and began to collect a list of errata which ran to nine or ten absolute howlers – all but one of them in the notes contributed by VALERIE ELIOT.

This exercised me so that I rang up MUNBY at the King's College Library, and told him that I'd like to see him and ask his opinion about this – I didn't know what to do about it. So he invited me over to lunch, and I went over today and showed him this list of errata – at which he raised his eyebrows.

I also showed him that VALERIE had quoted part of a letter that ELIOT had written to JOHN QUINN, the owner of the long-lost transcript, in which ELIOT urged him eloquently never to allow the unprinted parts of The Waste Land to be printed. This part of ELIOT's letter, although she quoted the first part, MRS. VALERIE ELIOT suppressed. This also struck MUNBY.

I said that I didn't know what to do; I thought of sending this list of mistakes to DU SAUTOY, but something would really have to be done about them. It's too late to correct them in this first edition, but they certainly must be corrected.

So MUNBY suggested that as he was writing to VALERIE ELIOT himself, he might act as a kind of go-between for me. I copied out the list of errata, he made a Xerox of it, and sent a copy.

After I came home I found the review of both The Waste Land and the SENCOURT book, by Helen Gardner, in this week's New Statesman – and that too exercised me! For one thing, the discrepancy in the price between the Faber edition and the Harcourt, Brace; the Faber edition apparently sells for £5 which is a little more than half the American price: $22.50 is exactly £9.

And here is the passage from ELIOT's letter to Quinn that she left out. Apparently it was the second time ELIOT brought the subject up and he said: "You will find a great many sets of verse (this is referring to typescript he's sending him) which have never been printed and which I am sure you will agree never ought to be printed and in putting them in your hands I beg you fervently to keep them to yourself and see that they never are printed."

It seems to me that this is a good deal more forceful a veto, or a statement of his preference, than is attached to his Will; and although VALERIE has every legal right to go ahead and print these unprintable verses in spite of what he said, it seems to me that her moral position on it is a bit wobbly.

November 17, [1971]

I have just written a letter to The Times which I don't intend to send – but I might one of these days. This is it:

Sir: As literary London must be aware by now, T. S. Eliot left an injunction forbidding his executor to 'facilitate or countenance' any biography of him. His executor, who is also his widow, has been most conscientious and exemplary in carrying out his wish: she has denied access to her husband's papers and even refused permission to quote from his published works; she has also persuaded most of Eliot's family and friends to have no commerce with any would-be biographer.

Mrs. Eliot knows, however, that this attitude is unrealistic and can only be temporary; she admits that a biography must one day be written, but she intends to choose – or at least insist on approving – the official biographer. Meantime she has been fully engaged in the pious task of preparing for the printer two memorials of her husband: his letters (which I understand we cannot hope to see for several years) and the Facsimile edition of <u>The Waste Land</u>, showing the 'editing' of it by Ezra Pound and reproducing all the verses and passages that were left out of the published poem.

This book has recently been vouchsafed us, in two identical Transatlantic editions, and has been widely hailed as a masterpiece of editing and a worthy tribute to her husband's memory. Is it in fact either?

A cursory reading of Mrs. Eliot's editorial notes (pp 125–131) reveals no less than seven misprints or errors of fact, the most egregious blunder being two misquotations in three lines from <u>The Love Song of J. Alfred Prufrock</u>.

In her introduction Mrs. Eliot quotes part of the letter written in 1922 from her husband to John Quinn, the New York lawyer to whom Eliot, in gratitude for Quinn's constant financial help, sent this unique transcript. Here is the continuation of the letter which Mrs. Eliot did not quote:

'Naturally, I hope that the portions which I have suppressed will never appear in print, and in sending them to you I am sending you the only copies of these parts.'

In another letter to Quinn, undoubtedly known to Mrs. Eliot, her husband wrote:

You will find a great many sets of verse which have never been printed and which I am sure you will agree never ought to be printed, and, in putting them in your hands, <u>I beg you fervently to keep them to yourself and see that they never are print</u> (italics mine).

Why did Mrs. Eliot find her husband's wishes so mandatory in one instance and, in the other, so easy to disregard? This is a question whose answer future biographers will be bound to raise.

I am, Sir, etc.

November 18, [1971]

PAT GARRATT reports as follows; that Faber has told her that the discrepancy in the price between the American and the British Facsimile edition of <u>The Waste Land</u> is explained as follows: there is a limited edition over here which sells at roughly £9 – the ordinary edition sells at £5; that the printing was done in this country and pages shipped to Harcourt. In short, the Oxford University printer gets all the credit, and if there's any blame attached, I supposed the blame, for any mistakes that are made in the text

I haven't compared them carefully, but I have picked up at Hoeffers the other day a copy of the £5 edition of <u>The Waste Land</u> and it seemed identical with the one I was sent from New York which cost $22.50 or £9.

I wonder what MR. JOVANOVICH's place in all this is?

Could it be that he has taken the cheaper of the two editions in from England, in effect, and charged the unwary public just double what it was worth. Could it be?

I wrote, but I have not yet posted, the following letter, to A. N. L. MUNBY:

> Dear Dr. Munby: My spies (there's only one, really) report the following, gleaned from Faber & Faber (right under their guns): (a) that there are two U.K. editions of The Waste Land Facsimile, one selling at £5 and a limited edition at £9 – same price as the US edition; (b) that the book was entirely printed in this country and sheets were imported by Harcourt for the US edition.
>
> These two pieces of intelligence raise two interesting points: Are Harcourt, Brace justified in their claim on the flyleaf of the US edition (printed in the United States of America) and in the price of $22.50 they have put on a book that is apparently identical with one that sells in Britain for £5? And since the Oxford Press did the printing of the book, must not Mr. Ridler (with Mrs. Eliot of course) bear his share of responsibility for the mistakes in it?
>
> I ain't said nothing to nobody – as yet – about these mistakes; and my anti-tenterhook muscles and nerves as well-developed, of necessity. But I can't help wondering what would happen if a letter to The Times laid all this – plus, perhaps, the stand-off at the Bodleian – before the public, or that small and violent part of it that reads letters to The Times? Mightn't one result, conceivably, be that the Bodleian might be shamed into making those papers accessible – or that Faber & Faber might give their permission to quote a reasonable amount of Eliot's published work?

Thoughts of a dry brain in a dry reason. Yours sincerely.

November 19, [1971]

Drove to Northamptonshire to Weston Hall to have lunch with the Sacheverell Sitwells. I got lost, of course, and it took me about three hours but I got there just in time for lunch.

A perfectly lovely old house which I hadn't remembered at all from seventeen years ago, and she obviously didn't remember me, but he did. He told me that there wasn't a word of truth in the report in the SENCOURT book that he and ELIOT had done a lot of sailing together – that he'd never sailed with him in his life; and he wasn't even aware that VIVIEN had a brother, let alone that his name was MAURICE. But he said he had seen quite a lot of ELIOT, and VIVIEN when they were first married, in about 1917 and for the next few years, and had often been to concerts with them in London. Then something happened, it just petered out; perhaps ELIOT dropped him.

He said he had told CYRIL CONNOLLY a few days before, and he was surprised CONNOLLY hadn't known about it, how ELIOT and VIVIEN met. I said I didn't know either. He said, "Well, they met on the river; she was playing a phonographs in a punt alongside his." I said, "Was it Henley or Oxford?" Oh well, he didn't know, but he assumed it was Oxford. It seems to me it was much more likely to have been HENLEY. Also this undetailed, unexplained meetings leaves out much more than it says, and is really tantalizing, it seems to me.

* * *

[Comment on a photograph showing VIRGINIA WOOLF, T. S. ELIOT and VIVIENNE.] VIVIENNE was a little creature, considerably shorter than either her husband or VIRGINIA WOOLF; she was wearing a cloche hat, looking down at the ground, her hands clasped in front of her, her toes pointed in, and her shoulders hunched. She looked miserable; she looked ill. That is the only picture of her I have seen.

November 20, [1971]

This morning I got a reply to my letter of November 16 to MICHAEL BALFOUR, the managing director of the Garnstone Press which published the SENCOURT book, and in which I had said: "I should be most grateful to you if you would answer one question which has been bothering me. Why did SENCOURT quote only two lines from ELIOT's published works? Under fair practice surely he might have quoted several hundred? This is not an idle question as you can see, for I shall be facing the same problem."

The answer came from DONALD ADAMSON, the man who finished the SENCOURT book, and who was asked to answer the letter by MR. BALFOUR. He says:

> The customary view of 'fair dealing' is, of course, that up to eight hundred words may be taken from a prose work (though only four hundred words in a single extract) and up to forty lines may be taken from a poem (though only if that does not exceed a quarter of the total poem). Robert Sencourt himself was under the impression that from the total of Eliot's writing he would be allowed to quote fifty lines of verse and a thousand words of prose. But when after his death I checked this with Faber & Faber, I was told there was no permission for quotations of any kind. In view of this it was decided to restrict quotations to the absolute minimum.

Well! As I said to MR. ADAMSON: "I should have thought there was a distinction between 'fair dealing' and 'permission to quote' but I am glad to have your explanation."

I also heard from MR. BALFOUR who said, "...a strange and fascinating situation?"

ANNE FOWLE has just rung up to say that she's going to try to get MAURICE HAIGH-WOOD, VIVIEN's brother to come and have drinks and meet me, and tell him why I want to meet him. What a hope!

November 23, 1971

I went to see MISS MARY TREVELYAN at her flat at No.23, Embankment Gardens, on the top floor. The windows look out over the gardens of the Chelsea Hospital, and the front windows over the river. She lived there, she told me, for twenty years — no, seventeen.

I was a little startled by her appearance; she might have been MICHAEL HORDERN in women's clothes. Very hearty, firm handshake, <u>bonhomme</u> or <u>faux bonhomme</u>? She reminded me of a line of ELIOT's — or rather one he lifted — "I would meet you upon this honestly."

She sat me down in the best chair, which she called the guest chair, by the fire, a high backed chair, very comfortable; and got us both drinks — whisky.

She was contemptuous and indignant about the SENCOURT book; obviously CHRISTOPHER SYKES. had it quite wrong about her being the one to 'hot up' JOHN HAYWARD in his spite against ELIOT. She spoke of ELIOT with great fondness, said that they were very good friends for twenty years, and that "he often sat in that chair where you're sitting."

She only met VALERIE once apparently; obviously no love lost there. She speaks almost with reverence of Dame HELEN GARDNER; uses some such phrase as, "...whose orders I'm taking." And she's willing to see anyone — but not prepared to say anything.

Then she said: "But I'll tell you in confidence..." and she proceeded to tell me something on which she enjoined absolute secrecy — which I'm only confiding in you, Dear

Diary – that she has a finished manuscript, now in Helen Gardner's hands, a memoir of her long friendship with ELIOT. She obviously would like to see it published, and hopes it will overbalance the misinformation and nasty insinuations of the SENCOURT book.

She was very vague about publication plans; and that poses a question: how can VALERIE countenance its appearance, or will HELEN GARDNER talks her round – or, possible, is Helen Gardner simply sitting on this book in order to suppress it, the way companies are supposed to buy up patents?

MISS TREVELYAN said that Spender's story of VALERIE being in the flat at the time when he broke the news about his wedding, to HAYWARD, is simply not true – but she didn't say what was true.

She seemed to like me, but I dare say that goes with all the boys. She scorned the idea of ELIOT's homosexuality. People hated him because they didn't understand what he was talking about. He was very funny [amusing] in private. She insisted on showing me out – waited on street till Pam appeared, seemed to like her too.

November 24, 1971

TSM'S NOTES FOR TOPIC A WHICH HAVE NOT BEEN RECORDED.

Oxford. RICHARD ELLMAN. Affable, impermeable, sympathetic) but unhelpful. Didn't know who biographer is to be, knows and likes VALERIE but also thinks there must be a biography written. Once wrote and offered TSE to write one but got fast turn-down. When during his life of Joyce there was a possibility he wouldn't get permission to quote, and decided to go ahead and write, that he could. We and his wife (sweet-faced woman in wheelchair) wished me luck and perhaps meant it. (Write to him)

SIR ISAIAH BERLIN. Received me in his cluttered H.Q. at Wolfson College, on the Banbury Road, gave me a glass of brown sherry (took none himself) and proceeded to regale me with a rapid-fire history of the revolt of the non-Fellows at Oxford, culminating in the founding of five new colleges – of which I think Wolfson is the latest to take the new Fellows. Very entertaining, very amused and amusing. I understood more than I have heretofore of his tumbling spate of words, by dint of keeping my good ear close to his mouth.

He took me over to the new "phoenix" building of St. Antony's, which the Wolfson people share (they won't have their own college till 1973). CARR, the WARDEN of St. Antony's (BILL DEAKIN's successor), a lean, twinkly historian, joined us for lunch and coffee afterwards. Over coffee I finally got a chance to speak my piece. BERLIN urged me on, said I could speak freely in front of Carr.

UNRECORDED NOTES FOR TOPIC A (contd.)

So I told them about the Bodleian papers, and my ill luck at finding a champion – including SPARROW. CARR went off to a meeting, and I unburdened myself to ISAIAH – but I hope discreetly. He himself of course can and will do nothing, but he was strongly of the opinion that I should meet HELEN GARDNER (we looked her up in the Oxford Who's Who and discovered she was a curator of the Bodleian, whereupon he said "No use!" – referring to the quest of the Bodleian papers. She's "very stubborn and very vain," according to B – but he still thought I should get ELLMANN ("a nice shy little man") to introduce me and then see whether an explosion was inevitable. I said I'd think it over.

November 25, 1971

I had lunch with CHRISTOPHER BRADBY at the Garrick. Sure enough, he turns out to be the brother of ANN RIDLER as I'd hoped. This came out in conversation; I didn't ask him.

He hadn't heard of my TSE project, and was inclined to be
skeptical at first, I think; but when we said goodbye he asked
me whether I wanted him to say anything about me to his sister
(I believe he was planning to telephone her this evening). I
said "Just tell her I'm the wonder of the western world – oh,
well, I'd better leave it to you. But I don't think I'll try to
see her just yet."

I told him I'd met TIM WILSON, his sister's son-in-law,
and was curious about the non-appearance in the Guardian
of his scheduled piece, which he had told me was to be on
the facsimile Waste Land and an interview with VALERIE,
and was to have appeared on November 8. (I had telephoned
the Guardian to ask what had happened and was told that the
piece had not come in.) BRADBY now told me that VALERIE, after
saying that she'd give TIM WILSON an interview, had "reneged"
– his word. I wonder why.[53]

– and, when I got home:

November 30, [1971]

MAURICE HAIGH-WOOD (first impressions): Tall (6ft 2?), thin,
grey (hair and moustache), well-nosed, slightly retreating
chin emphasised by elderly wattle; heavy-lidded eyes, skopaic
eye brows.

Soft-spoken, shy, conservative, a stockbroker. Seemed
about to apologise to me for not answering a letter he never
got. Accepted with alacrity my invitation to lunch next week
at the Garrick. After lunch, in Chink's study, he seemed to
accept everything I told him – about what I'm doing, about
TSE.'s veto, VALERIE, the ELIOT family and friends. Said he
had talked to SENCOURT and "corrected" what SENCOURT had
wrongly reported about his sister, seemed to feel he could do
the same for me.

---

53 The Wilson interview was published in *The Observer* and in a longer version in the US magazine *Esquire*.

December 3, 1971

Today I made my first foray into King's College Library by arrangement with DR. A. N. L. MUNBY, the Librarian. I got there about half past nine in the morning, and MUNBY was expecting me. He who was the Curator, not only of the Library, but of the HAYWARD Collection. This is one of the three main ammunition dumps of TSE papers.

MUNBY and I had already had some talk about the accessibility of parts of this collection, and we had agreed that I was to see everything that I legally could, and agreed that I would refrain from trying to get anything that I was forbidden by ELIOT's veto from seeing. He had quite a lot of stuff waiting for me, gave me a room to myself, and left me. I worked there all morning, then had lunch, by invitation, with him, in the Hall, now a cafeteria, and did as much as I could again in the afternoon, and then left, with an appointment to come back the following week.

In one of the manilla envelopes of miscellaneous stuff I found a visiting card of MRS. T. S. ELIOT, with this written on the reverse—not in ELIOT's writing (there was no date but the address was 68, Clarence Gate Gardens, Regents Park, N.W.1.). And this was written on the card:

> I am so sorry I missed seeing you this afternoon, ['this afternoon' crossed out, and 'last Friday' put in]. Thank you for the nice flower in pot. I do hope you will come and see me one day. Will you?

No signature and no address, but I couldn't help feeling it had been written by VIVIENNE to her husband after one of his visits to her, perhaps at the hospital, perhaps at home? On the 27th November, PAM's eagle eye had spotted in the Daily Telegraph this notice:

> Haigh-Wood. On November 26, suddenly, hospital, Ahme, beloved wife of Maurice Haigh, devoted mother

of Charles, and grandmother of Jane and Ann. Private funeral. Flowers to E.B. Ashton & Co., 96, Fulham Road, S.W.3., or donations, if desired, to Cancer Research.

I telephoned my researcher, PAT GARRATT, and asked her if she could find out something from the undertaker, E.B. Ashton & Co. She was unable to find out any addresses, but very foolishly, I thought, left mine with him.

Here are a few of my gleanings from my first session at the King's College Library. An example of one of ELIOT's practical jokes: A letter signed 'Town Clerk', announcing to the Faber Directors that an equestrian statue by A. J. MUNNINGS, and including figures of all the Directors, was to be erected at the corner of Russell Square and Thornhaugh Street. "It is proposed that concrete should be used for the group, marble being too expensive a medium for the purpose."

Note on health: In a letter to DESMOND MCCARTHY in November 1947, he speaks of two recent hernia operations, and "the sudden decision to have all my teeth out."

Note on Oxford: "My only trophy, a pewter mug, obtained from stroking a College junior four, at a time when all the real oarsmen were fighting for England and France."

As a blurb writer: I saw ten Faber & Faber catalogues, from 1937 to 1953, and 84 of the blurbs were initialed in pencil by ELIOT.

From a letter of recommendation from his tutor at Merton, HAROLD H. JOACHIM, dated July 1915: "I am quite sure that he would make a most successful teacher, and that he would deserve to win the affection as well as the respect of his pupils."

Note on law breaking: A summons dated 2nd October 1916, issued against THOMAS ELLIOTT (with two l's and two t's) aged 30, of 18, Crawford Mansions, Crawford Street. "For not sufficiently reducing the light as required by the Defence of the Realm Act."

In several references in letters to ELIOT from an old police constable, Janes, referring to MRS. ELIOT, VIVIENNE. The first, September 1934: "I have not heard from MRS. ELIOT so do not know where she his." Another: "I have not seen or heard from MRS. ELIOT since last November so do not know where she his." And a last: "I have not seen or heard from MRS. ELIOT since she came last Sunday week and took away the tin base."

December 4, [1971]

Wrote to ARCHIBALD MACLEISH, thanking him for his promise to write me something about ELIOT as soon as he has time. To FATHER CALLAN, Librarian of Milton Academy, thanking him for sending me a copy of an address ELIOT had made at the school; and to PROFESSOR EDOUARD RODITI, visiting French Professor at the University of California, at Santa Cruz, thanking him for his latest letter in which he promises to send me Xeroxes of a couple of ELIOT letters.

December 7, [1971]

Drove to Cambridge after breakfast and spend the day in King's College Library. My second go at the HAYWARD papers. Today was mostly pretty dry stuff: Thoughts after Lambeth, The Idea of a Christian Society, Church, Community and State, and a terrible pamphlet, Reunion by Destruction, reflections of a scheme for Church union in South India, a real dusty answer. But there were a few lighter-hearted bits and pieces. One was a letter to The Times, dated April, 1947. I wonder if it was ever printed; I'll have to check it.

> Sir: The voice of the bittern (vulgarly called by the rustics of Holt, Norfolk, among whom I passed my youth, the bumpshit) was distinctly heard at this address this afternoon at 6.50. Its springtime note, indicative of the mating season, was audible to

several observers and listeners. Among the rustics of Holt, Norfolk, among whom I passed my youth, this note, if heard before the middle of April, indicates a benign summer and a prolific harvest.

I am, Sir, You obedient servant, John Hayward.

(but apparently written by TSE). Also one stanza, which I won't repeat here, of the much talked about Old King Bolo's Big Black Queen.

The Christmas vacation had begun, so the Library was locked up from 1 to 2.15 p.m. – with me inside it. If I had had the equipment, and knew where to look for the papers, I might have been tempted to – but I didn't, so I wasn't.

December 8, [1971]

Letter from FRANCES LINDLEY, my New York Editor: "The Bodleian episode is shocking. I asked our resident legal adviser for a suggestion as to the next step and he advised getting hold of some person or persons with more clout than the abominable Hunt, rather than trying to make a legal issue of it. Your solicitor friend may have quite other ideas, of course. I seriously hope you are keeping a record of these attempts to keep you from finding out where the body is buried, not least because it seems more and more obvious that somebody is, in fact, buried somewhere. It is beginning to sound hideously like Hobhouse & Kinneard contriving to have Byron's memoirs burned."

And here is the letter I have written today to WILLIAM FRANKEL, my barrister friend, now Editor of The Jewish Chronicle:

> Dear William: Here is my draft of the proposed letter to the Librarian of the Bodleian. I've just heard from my New York Editor on the subject. (And then I repeat a paragraph of her letter).

I think I know someone in Oxford with more clout who would probably like to weigh in: John Sparrow, Warden of All Souls', who is also an ex-barrister. But I don't think I'd like to have him on my side. For one thing he's an enemy, or at least a great detractor, of Eliot. I await your comments and suggestions.

And here is the letter to the Bodleian Librarian:

Dear Mr. Shackleton: I am a senior member of the University, being a Master of Arts at New College. As such, I believe I have the rights and privileges of a reader at the Bodleian. I have been commissioned by Harper & Row, New York publishers, to write a biography of T. S. Eliot. Macmillans, of London, are also interested and have taken an option on the book. I tell you this to show that my interest in T. S. Eliot is serious and that my qualifications to be his biographer are thought to be sufficient.

I have seen a copy of the first Mrs. Eliot's will. Paragraph 5 reads as follows: (and then I given him the paragraph). None of these conditions forbids a serious student to see and read these papers, yet I was told by one of your colleagues when I applied to the Bodleian on November 24 that he would not allow anyone to see them until everyone concerned is dead. Furthermore, that if the existence of these papers becomes widely known, they will probably be placed under the protection of the present Mrs. Eliot. When I asked by what right the Library thus sequestered these papers, your colleague replied, in effect, that libraries can make their own rules in such matters. May I inquire whether this opinion has your approval and support? Yours faithfully,

December 9 & 10, [1971]

I spent parts of both of these days at the King's College Library, going through the HAYWARD Collection.

December 8, 1971

Went to London and had lunch with SIR ALEC RANDALL at the Garrick. SIR ALEC was a dusty, donnish, ex-Foreign Office man, with long service in Rome, Rumania and the Balkans, whose principal interest at present, he tells me, is a study of the relationship between the Papacy and the Italian Government in the late 19th century. He's a great admirer of PIO Nonc.

His connection with ELIOT was that he reviewed the German books for both The Criterion and The Times Literary Supplement and he'd met ELIOT through Richmond, the Editor of the TLS. He says he never knew him well. He was shocked apparently when I told him the peak circulation of The Criterion (a figure which ELIOT had once told me) – nine hundred.

SIR ALEC didn't know VIVIEN, or that she wrote for The Criterion. He says he has some letters from ELIOT on Criterion business; he doesn't seem to think they're very interesting but he'll took them over in case I might find they're any use. A nice man; not much help I fear.

December 9, 1971

Lunch again at the Garrick with MAURICE HAIGH-WOOD, VIVIEN's long sought (by me) brother; and a long awaited, almost unhoped-for occasion. Alas, nothing whatever came of it. The acoustics in the dining room at the Garrick are very poor; HAIGH-WOOD is a fearfully shy man and almost inaudible; and to make everything worse he spilt some avocado vinaigrette on his front, which I attempted not to notice but which nearly knocked him out, and he spent the next fifteen minutes surreptitiously trying to remove the traces. A nice old 'dull doggie'; I should say not very perceptive, and he says he can't remember anything.

He lived outside the country most of the time his sister and ELIOT were married, about eight years in Italy; he loves Rome, knew Prodwell. His parents honeymooned in Venice in pre-Lido days, and went picnicking there. They couldn't understand the frantic arm-waving by distant police but finally got the message that it was an artillery range when a shell whooshed overhead:

HAIGH-WOOD is very shy, nearly inaudible. He did say with some emphasis that he saw his sister shortly before she died and that she was no more mad than he was.

I didn't attempt to ask him any questions but I did sound him out on the Bodleian papers. He knew about them but had no idea who now owns the copyright or who his sister's executor is. VALERIE had sent him a copy of the Waste Land Facsimile, so I take it that he is on friendly terms with her, if not in her camp.

I asked him if he would like to come down for a weekend and he said that after Christmas he would; he is spending Christmas with his grandchildren. I think he misses his wife very much.

Last night I dreamed about JOHN HAYWARD, or at least JOHN HAYWARD came into my dream. The dream seemed almost like a vision because I woke up with tears in my eyes, because in the dream the children had loved him; I realized the children were right – I must remember this.

December 12, [1971]

I have come across the following passages in BERTRAND RUSSELL's autobiography: In Volume 1, page 212:

> The students, as I said before, were admirable. I had a postgraduate class of twelve who used to come to tea with me once a week. One of them was

T. S. Eliot, who subsequently wrote a poem about it, called Mr. Apollinax. I did now know at the time that ELIOT wrote poetry. He had, I think, already written Portrait of a Lady and Prufrock, but he did not see fit to mention the fact. He was extraordinarily silent and only once made a remark which struck me. I was praising Heraclitus, and he observed: 'Yes, he always reminds me of Villon.' I thought this remark so good that I always wished he would make another.

One day, in October 1974, I met T. S. Eliot in New Oxford Street. I did not know he was in Europe, but I found he had come to England from Berlin. I naturally asked him what he thought of the War.

'I don't know,' he replied. 'I only know that I am not a pacifist.' That is to say, he considered any excuse good enough for homicide.

I became great friends with him, and subsequently with his wife, whom he married early in 1915. As they were desperately poor, I lent them one of the two bedrooms in my flat, with the result that I saw a great deal of them. I was fond of them both and endeavoured to help them in their troubles, until I discovered that their troubles were what they enjoyed. I held some debentures, nominally worth £3,000, in an engineering firm which, during the war, naturally took to making munitions. I was much puzzled in my conscience as to what to do with these debentures, and at last I gave them to Eliot. Years afterwards, when the war was finished, and he was no longer poor, he gave them back to me.

---

*The suggestion sometimes made, however, that one of us influenced the other, is without foundation.

Page 33, two years later, 1916:

> I had gone up to London for the day from Bosham in Sussex, where I was staying with the Eliots. I had to get them to bring up my brush and comb and toothbrush, because the Government objected to my fetching them myself.

In BERTRAND RUSSELL's Autobiography I found some interesting facts about ELIOT's first marriage. From a letter from RUSSELL to LADY OTTOLINE MORRELL, dated July, 1915:

> Friday evening I dined with my Harvard pupil, Eliot, and his bride. I expected her to be terrible, from his mysteriousness, but she was not so bad. She is light, a little vulgar, adventurous, full of life; an artist, I think he said, but I should have thought her an actress. He is exquisite and listless. She says she married him to stimulate him, but finds she can't do it. Obviously, he married in order to be stimulated. I think she will soon be tired of him. She refuses to go to America to see his people, for fear of submarines. He is ashamed of his marriage, and very grateful if one is kind to her. He is the 'Miss Sands' type of American.

(MISS SANDS was a highly cultivated New Englander, a painter, and a friend of HENRY JAMES and LOGAN PEARSALL SMITH.)

From another letter, postmarked November 10, 1915:

> Eliot had a half holiday yesterday and got home at 3.30. It is quite funny how I have come to love him, as if he were my son. He is becoming much more of a man. He has a profound and quite unselfish devotion to

his wife, and she is really very fond of him, but has
impulses of cruelty to him from time to time. It is a
Dostoevsky kind of cruelty, not a straightforward,
everyday kind. I am every day getting things more
right between them, but I can't let them alone at
present, and of course I, myself, get very much
interested. She is a person who lives on a knife edge,
and will end as a criminal or a saint; I don't know
which yet. She has a perfect capacity for both.

On page 58, a letter from ELIOT to BERTRAND RUSSELL, in January, 1916:

Dear Bertie: This is wonderfully kind of you; really
the last straw, so to speak, of generosity. I am very
sorry you have to come back, and Vivienne says you
have been an angel to her; but of course I shall jump
at the opportunity with the utmost gratitude. I am
sure you have done everything possible, and handled
her in the very best way; better than I. I often wonder
how things would have turned out but for you. I
believe we shall owe her life to you, even.
   * Mrs. Eliot was ill and needed a holiday. Eliot,
at first, could not leave London, so I went first with
her to Torquay, and Eliot replaced me after a few days.

The ELIOTs were then living in BERTRAND RUSSELL's flat. On the same page, a letter from ELIOT's mother, Charlotte C. ELIOT, from St. Louis, to RUSSELL:

I am sure your influence, in every way, will confirm
my son in his choice of Philosophy as a life work.
Professor Wood speaks of his thesis as being of
exceptional value. I had hoped he would seek a
university appointment next year; if he does not,
I shall feel regret. I have absolute faith in his

philosophy, but not in the vers libre. Tom is very grateful to you for your sympathy and kindness. This gratitude I share.

Page 74, a letter from RUSSELL to OTTOLINE MORRELL, September, 1916:

I shall soon have come to the end of the readjustment with Mrs. E. (Mrs. Eliot). I think it will be all right on a better basis. AS soon as it is settled, I will come to Garsington. I long to come.

Page 173, a letter from ELIOT to RUSSELL, dated October 15, 1923:

Dear Bertie: I was delighted to get your letter. It gives me very great pleasure to know that you like The Waste Land, and especially Part V, which, in my opinion, is not only the best part, but the only part that justifies the whole, at all. It means a great deal to me that you like it. I must tell you that eighteen months ago, before it was published anywhere, Vivienne wanted me to send you the manuscript to read because she was sure that you were one of the very few persons who might possibly see anything in it. But we felt that you might prefer to have nothing to do with us. It is absurd to say that we wished to drop you. Vivienne has had a frightful illness, and nearly died in the spring, as Ottoline has probably told you, and that she has been in the country ever since. She has not yet come back.
    Dinner is rather difficult for me at present, but might I come to tea with you on Saturday? I should like to see you very much: there have been many times when I have thought that. Yours ever, TSE

Another letter, dated the 21st April 1925:

Dear Bertie: If you are still in London, I should very much like to see you. My times and places are very restricted, but it is unnecessary to mention them unless I hear from you. I want words from you which only you can give, but if you have now ceased to care at all about either of us, just write on a slip, 'I do not care to see you', or, 'I do not care to see either of you', and I will understand. In case of that, I will tell you now that everything has turned out as you predicted ten years ago. You are a great psychologist. Yours, TSE

From another letter, dated 7th May, 1925:

My dear Bertie: Thank you very much indeed for your letter. As you say, it is very difficult for you to make suggestions until I can see you. For instance, I don't know to what extent the changes which have taken place, since we were in touch with you, would seem to you material. What you suggest seems to me, of course, what should have been done years ago. Since then her health is a thousand times worse. Her only alternative would be to live quite alone, if she could. And the fact that living with me has done her so much damage, does not help me to come to any decision. I need the help of someone who understands her. I find her still perpetually baffling and deceptive. She seems to me like a child of six, with an immensely clever and precocious mind. She writes extremely well – stories, etc. – in great originality; and I can never escape from the spell of her persuasive, even coercive, gift of argument.

    Well, thank you very much Bertie. I feel quite desperate. I hope to see you in the autumn. Yours ever, TSE

Then there is a great gap. In Volume 3, on page 53, there is an exchange of letters on June, 1949, from ELIOT to RUSSELL, apparently on the occasion of RUSSELL's being given the Order of Merit; to which RUSSELL replied in a short note. He did permit himself one little dig: "... In old days, when we were huddled together in RUSSELL Chambers, we could hardly have expected that lapse of time would make us so respectable...."

This 1964 farewell from ELIOT, addressed to The Right Honourable EARL RUSSELL, O. M.:

> Dear Bertie: My wife and I listened the other night to your broadcast interview and thought it went over extremely well. As you may know, I disagree with your views on most subjects, but I thought that you put your beliefs over in a most dignified, and even persuasive way. I wanted you to know this as you are getting on so far; and as I, myself, am, I hope, somewhat mellowed by age. With grateful and affectionate memories, Yours ever, Tom.

December 17, [1971]

Went to King's and read all morning, and for part of the afternoon:

> A broadcast by Eliot, 1941, Towards a Christian Britain – an unexceptionable, almost meaningless pi-jaw; Savonarola, the long dramatic poem by his mother, Charlotte Eliot, with an introduction by him, in which he covered up what he thought of the poem pretty well; and introduction by Eliot to The Wheel of Fire by Wilson McKnight; a Memoir of his on Irving Babbitt; introduction to the Selected Poems of Marianne Moore; and a very French novel called Bubu of Montparnasse by Charles Louis Phillipe, to which he had also written a preface.

Today I also got a letter from Moshe Perlman, from Jerusalem, to whom I have owed a letter for a long time, but dear Moish had sent me, as a coal of fire, a long piece on Eliot and anti-Semitism, from the Jewish magazine, Commentary.

December 18, [1971]

Drove to Cambridge before light, and spent the day at King's College Library. DR. MUNBY treated me to lunch for the second time in the Hall, with coffee afterwards in the S.C.R. I looked mostly at introduction by ELIOT: to CHARLES BAUDELAIRE's Intimate Journals; to WILKIE COLLINS' Moonstone; to an anthology called The Little Book of Modern Verse by ANN RIDLER; a selection of JOYCE's prose; a war book edited by STORM JAMIESON, contributions by thirty-two writers, including a very prosaic and pedestrian poem by ELIOT, of which I copied down the last two stanzas; introduction to CHARLES WILLIAMS' All Hallows' Eve; and a speech by WILLIAM R. CASSELL at the 50th Anniversary Dinner of the Fox Club, one of ELIOT's undergraduate clubs at Harvard, containing A Ballad of the Fox Dinner by ELIOT, written for the Diner of 1909 (some of his fellow members were CABOT LODGE, BEN WHITE BROOKS, NORRIS WILLIAMS, the tennis player, and HERMAN HAGEDORN, who was much regarded as a poet); an introduction to A Portrait of Michael Roberts; to a book on Lawrence by FATHER WILLIAM TIVERTON; to Thoughts for Meditation, a collection by an Indian named N. GANGOULEE; a 1931 anthology of college verse called Cap and Gown, containing one poem by ELIOT, reprinted from The Harvard Advocate (other contributors were JOHN PEALE BISHOP, EDMUND WILSON, NIVEN BUSCH, SCHUYLER JACKSON and BALFOUR DANIELS); a collection of Third Programme talks called From the Third Programme, edited by JOHN MORRIS, in which ELIOT's contribution was Virgil and the Christian World (not as dull as it sounds).

I saw photographs of a presentation goblet given to GEOFFREY FABER on the occasion of his Knighthood, by his

fellow directors on Faber & Faber, and incised on the side of
the goblet was a poem by ELIOT:

> Amazed astronomers did late descry
> A new great luminary in the sky.
> Straight to the Queen the prompt petition came:
> 'Would she be pleased to give this star a name?'
> 'Sir Geoffrey, let it be.' Her word benign
> The Heavens approved, and all the Muses nine.

Then, finally, a photograph book of London, got out in 1953, called <u>Gala Day in London</u>, with text by JOHN BETJEMAN, PAUL DANE, CLIFFORD DIAMOND, ELIOT, LAURIE LEE, etc., etc. Most of them contributed more than one verse or caption; but ELIOT only one, opposite the fifth photograph, of a cat crouched on a park bench:

> Let quacks, empirics, dolts, debate
> The quandaries of Church and State.
> Let intellectuals address
> The latest cultural congress.
> Here is the true contemplative;
> Content to live, perhaps let live.
> The sage, disposed to sit and stare,
> With a vacant mind, in a vacant square.

And today I got a reply from RUSSELL KIRK, in Mecosta, Michigan, who is apparently writing a book on ELIOT, which will be out next month or so, of which he promises to send me a copy or proofs, and also photostats of a good many letters from ELIOT.

December 18, 1971

A letter from MAURICE HAIGH-WOOD:

> Dear Matthews: It was very good of you to write, and
> in fact you have put coals of fire on my head, as it is

I who should have written before now to thank you for a most enjoyable lunch.

It is most kind of you to ask me for a weekend later on, and I shall very much hope to be able to come, especially to such a delightful part of the world.

No doubt you have read what the. critics have had to say about the original Waste Land and also about poor old Sencourt's Memoir. A good deal of what Valerie Eliot has written in her introduction to the original Waste Land was unknown to me. I was away in the War from 1919 to 1919 and then went to live and work in Italy at the end of 1924. I was in Italy nearly all the time from then until 1932 (and in the War again 1939 to 1945).

Thank you very much indeed for your and your wife's most kind wishes, which I warmly reciprocate. Yours sincerely, Maurice Haigh-Wood.

Same day:

I have written, but not sent, the following letter to DR. DONALD GALLUP, of Yale. (I may or may not sent it):

Dear Dr. Gallup: I seem to remember your telling me (and with a slight smile) that publication of the Facsimile Waste Land had been postponed because Valerie Eliot was determined that the book should be a flawless piece of scholarship. As a professional scholar, you knew what a counsel of perfection that was. Or so I interpreted your smile.

By this time you must have perused the book with some care, and will therefore have discovered the dragon's teeth of errors, mostly in the editorial notes, pp.125-130. I could hardly believe my proof reader's eyes when they spotted the first one, and then led me on to the second, third, etcetera. My discovery dates back to some weeks ago, when I was first looking over the book. I didn't know what to do about it, but I thought something should be done; so I took my marked copy of the Facsimile <u>Waste Land</u> to Dr. A. N. L. Munby, the Librarian of King's College, Cambridge, who I am sure you know. He was about to write to Mr. Du Sautoy, the head of Faber & Faber, and suggested that he might include a copy of my list of errors. He did so; whether or not he had a reply from Mr. Du Sautoy I don't know, but he did hear from Valerie Eliot, who was apparently annoyed that I hadn't sent my list to her. I really was too embarrassed to do that, no matter what she thinks my motives were. I can only imagine the chagrin she must be feeling: especially in view of the encomiums she has received in the press on her meticulous editing. Either no one else has noticed the errors or there is a conspiracy of silence on her behalf, for I have seen no mention of it in the papers.

You will know (I don't) what the size of the edition was and what the chances are of there being a second edition, in which these errors can be corrected. The reason I am sending my list to you is merely to cover the unlikely possibility that you have not already spotted everything that appears on my list; and because I regard you as the even-handed umpire (though you may be neutral against me) in the Tsetse War, unto whom all hearts are open, all desires known, and from whom no secrets are hid.

There are two questions about the Facsimile edition that I hope you can and will answer for me: (1) Why does the US edition bear the legend 'Printed in the United States of America' (surely the whole thing was printed at Oxford and sheets were imported?) (2) Why does the US edition sell for $22.50 when an apparently identical edition in the U. K. sells for £5.00?

My list of errors is on a separate page. Yours sincerely,

December 21, 1971

I've just had a telephone conversation with MRS. IGOR VINOGRADOFF. She was OTTOLINE MORRELL's daughter, and a friend of AD LUBBOCK, who put me on to her, and I wrote and asked her if I could talk to her about her memories of T. S. ELIOT when he visited her mother's house at Garsington.

She told me on the telephone when I said I hope she wasn't in VALERIE ELIOT's camp, that she isn't in anybody's camp but she doesn't think that she knows enough to make it worth while to talk to me about ELIOT because she was only a girl of fourteen. She said she had listened to him talking but he wasn't aware of her at all.

I said, "That's fine because you were watching _him_." But she said, "No, no; but I have got some marvellous photographs – albums of them." So I said, "Well, Lord, I'd go to Kamchatka for that!"

So the upshot of it is that she's invited me for lunch. She lives somewhere near Banbury and I'm to go over there on the 11th January to see these photographs

I must say that I dreamed last night that I had written all but the last two chapters of a book I was writing – not this book, I think, but _a_ book – the deadline was staring me in the face, and I had a feeling of absolute physical cowardice about not being able to finish it. I don't know whether that's an omen or not.

The day before yesterday we had a number of people to lunch including the STEPHEN RYDERS, and young CHARLES RYDER brought a friend of his along. I never did get his name – I suppose he was an old Etonian – but he looked a bit older than that and turned out to be a barrister. He asked me about the ELIOT book, and it turned out that he is, or claims to be, VALERIE ELIOT's barrister. I talked to him at some length and I _hope_, but only _hope_, not indiscreetly!

I can't believe that he's very close to her, however, as he had never even heard of JABEZ SMITH, who was the solicitor for ELIOT, and I think drew up his Will.

A letter today from MRS. OAKELEY, JOHN HAYWARD's sister, who had told me that she was going to try to track down the French housekeeper that HAYWARD and ELIOT had at the time of their bust-up. The letter is as follows:

Dear Mr. Matthews: I think I had better get all this off to you before all the grandchildren arrive etc. on Tuesday. I visited Mrs. Thompson yesterday, (69 Longridge Road, Earls Court). She is 88 but bright as a button although rather dim-sighted. She worked at 19 Carlisle Mansions until 1948 when she was of retiring age and her legs were 'bad': but she continued to do sewing jobs for my brother and therefore used to call in to see him from time to time. She hunted through her address book but could not find Madame's name, but she says she will try and remember it. She says it was not a French name and she believes that Madame had been married to an Englishman. Madame left after Mr. Eliot's marriage when my brother really needed a man's help, and she started a boarding-house, so Mrs. Thompson told me, near Lotts Road, Chelsea (I remember my brother told me that Madame had asked for a large galvanized dustbin as a parting present! So that explains it). I asked Mrs. T. if my brother had told her anything about Mr. Eliot's marriage. She said 'Oh, it came as a complete surprise. Mr. Eliot did not inform him that he was getting married. They were married at 6 a.m. just around the corner at St. Barnabas' Church and then flew over to Nice for the honeymoon. I asked if she had been told how the news was broken, and she said she did not know. "I had very little help from William Askwith's sister, but she thought that Mrs. Lines' Agency might be able to help trace Madame. Mrs. Lines' Employment Agency in High Street, Kensington was co-operative and took particulars in case they could trace as far back as 1948. I said I would pay for any help they could give as the result of their investigations.

There is another housekeeper still alive who was with John for about six years I think before the War. She left because of her 'feet' but has apparently kept up with Mrs. Thompson. She is Miss Scarth, 27 Mansfield Road, Tweedmouth, Berwick-on-Tweed. I do not remember her, but of course I was abroad for many years.

I have not got round to exploring the boarding-houses in or around Lotts Road, and am not quite sure how one sets about this, but that seems to be the next step.

I am sorry my visits have not been more fruitful. Yours sincerely, Diana Oakeley.

December 22, [1971]

(the shortest day of the year – though they all seem that way now) A letter from NEVILL COGHILL; a note, reading as follows:

No scholar could possibly blame you for seeking the truth, as a biographer. At the same time there is a load of things I am ashamed of in my life, and would not wish to be dug up after my death; so I can sympathize with the Eliot family view, too. I hope you will pursue your researches, and find nothing but what is laudable and lovable; but I think Eliot was difficult to love, and Bertrand Russell impossible. I knew one of his sons, who spat at the mention of his name – but I must admit I didn't much like the son either. Peace be with them all. I wish you a happy Christmas, and great success with your book. One so scrupulous as you have shown yourself to be, cannot got wrong.

December 23, 1971

Well, I've written to MISS SCARTH and asked her if she can remember Madame's name so that I can make enquiries about the boarding-house, or get PAT GARRAT to trace her boarding-house near Lots Road. I have also sent that letter to DR. GALLUP because I decided I would, and today I had a letter from FRANCES LINDLEY strongly urging me to do it – I've already done it – and saying that she would love to see the list of errors, so I sent for those.

December 23, [1971]

Here's what might be called 'an interesting development'. In a letter to me, dated 10th June, 1970, MRS. ELIOT wrote: "In his Will, or rather, in a memorandum with it, my husband said I was neither to 'facilitate nor countenance' the writing of a biography; and as his sole executrix, I must carry out his wishes."

My researcher, MISS PATRICIA GARRETT, got me a copy of ELIOT's Will from Somerset House, but there was no such memorandum attached to it. This morning I had a letter from her, dated December 21, saying as follows:

> I have now had a word with the solicitor who handled the Will of TSE – a Mr. Jabez Smith, of Herbert Oppenheimer, Nathan & van Dyke, of Copthall Avenue, E.C. 2. He was most forthcoming, and said that at no time did Eliot ever issue legally binding instructions to his executors, forbidding them to help biographers. "I know he (TSE) expressed the wish that no one should write a biography about him. Mrs. Eliot will not help anyone in this respect, but I would be surprised if there were any means of stopping anyone doing so. He expressed this wish in a conversation with me, and, I think, in a letter to

his wife." (Mr. Jabez Smith can be contacted on 01-628 9611 – and he will be contacted.)

<u>Later</u>: I have just had a telephone conversation with MR. JABEZ SMITH who was, as PAT GARRETT said in her letter, quite forthcoming, and sympathetic, and repeated his statement that if ELIOT had ever made a memorandum, it didn't come through the act of probating the will, which apparently cuts out what lawyers regard as irrelevant matters; and that in his opinion, there was nothing legally binding about the memorandum, in any case. But I said: "What about copyright?" At which he said: "Of course, yes, of course." (I don't know whether he had failed to think of that, or not.) I said, would there be any way of legally proceeding in order to get hold of this forbidden material? And at this point, he said he couldn't give me any legal advice, but he offered to have a word with MRS. ELIOT. I told him I had already, in effect, had several words with MRS. ELIOT, and that I would be no use. He then told me that she had broken her arm, and I said I was very sorry.

December 24, [1971]

At the risk of possibly repeating myself, I want to get the complete record of the opposition I am encountering to doing the ELIOT; so I am going back on my tracks and will quote from several letters that I have received.

The first is from the secretary of a partner, or former partner, of Faber & Faber, MR. MORLEY KENNERLEY. I wrote to him rather reluctantly, but at the urgent suggestion of a friend of mine, DAVID FOOTMAN, who seemed to be certain that MR. KENNERLEY would at least reply to me, and probably see me. The reply I got, as I say, was from his secretary, MISS KATHLEEN ASH, who told me that MR. KENNERLEY was very ill with pneumonia, and that "there is an added complication to your request for an interview to talk about MR. ELIOT, and that is that he, MR. ELIOT, was very much against having

a book written about him, and did in fact forbid this in
his Will. As MR. KENNERLEY was a very old friend of MR.
ELIOT's, he would feel it impossible to go against MR. ELIOT's
wishes in the matter of a biography, as I'm sure you will
understand."

Next I will refer to the only two letters I have had so far
from MRS. T. S. ELIOT; the first dated 10th June, 1970, in which
she says:

> I cannot give you access to papers of letters, and
> permission to quote would be refused.

And in a second letter, dated 19th June, 1970, she says:
> Yes, the Hayward Papers are out of bounds; the
> family will not co-operate either.

These two statements are only partly true—some of the
HAYWARD Papers are out of bounds, not only to me, but to her,
and to everybody. But others, I have been given access to.
As for the family not co-operating, it depends on who you
mean by the family, and who considers themselves family.
Before I had heard from MRS. ELIOT that the family would not
co-operate, I had written on June 1, 1970, in good faith, to
the only member of the ELIOT family I knew, MRS. THEODORE
STURTEVANT, in Newport, asking her to tell me everything
she could remember about her cousin TOM. And she (also not
realising that she was breaking the ELIOT law) replied to
me on June 30th at considerable length. Whether I shall ever
be able to use any of what she told me, I don't know, but for
this particular record I am going to put down her memories
of VIVIENNE ELIOT, T. S. ELIOT's first wife, whom she met on a
visit to London in 1922.

I am now quoting from her letter:

> I was twelve, and we went to tea with Cousin Tom
> and Vivienne. I had just been reading a gorgeously

illustrated edition of The Idylls of the King, where Vivienne was a gorgeous, auburn-haired, romantically dressed beauty; and expected that the new cousin I was about to meet, must have a wife who looked like Tennyson's Vivienne. To my great confusion, Cousin Tom's wife was very thin, pale, and her face was surrounded by masses of soft black clouds of hair. She was silent and fragile, and totally unaware of me. She rather repelled and frightened me; she was strange.

I can't separate what I saw and felt from what I may have overheard my parents saying later. There seemed to be all sorts of problems and worries about Vivienne, and something about Cousin Tom and Pa. All of these vague memories by a twelve-year-old are valueless; just gossipy inaccuracies. The only clear and true memory is that I did feel something mysterious and strange in Vivienne; and that Cousin Tom was trying very hard in some way; and that he liked me.

I have now written my solicitor, COLIN OLIVER, in London, asking him for an appointment on December 31. I want to ask him two things: VALERIE ELIOT's legal position, vis-à-vis me; and, what my legal rights are, if any, about those papers at the Bodleian.

December 30, [1971]

This morning, two letters: one from MARJORIE WEINER, my London agent, who had already telephoned me about a BBC programme, to take place next week, on <u>The Mysterious Mr. Eliot</u>. Her letter says, in part:

>...There was probably no ukase in the Eliot Will against radio or T.V. Many people just overlook this,

and it has formed a good loophole. I also thought that the fact that a programme is being made has redoubled the ban on the book. Maybe the BBC don't want it until the programme is shown.

I'm afraid I don't altogether understand this.

The second letter was from HERBERT OPPENHEIMER, NATHAN and VAN DYKE, from MR. A. R. JABEZ-SMITH:

I find that I misinformed you when I told you on the telephone recently, that T. S. Eliot had only expressed orally his strong objection to the writing of his biography. I have since looked at a memorandum he left with his Will, which deals with a number of unrelated matters, but does include the following: 'I do not wish my Executors to facilitate or countenance the writing of any biography of me.

This memorandum was not the subject of probate with the Will, as the court will not give probate to any document which is not directly concerned with the disposal of the deceased's estate. It is, however, a memorandum which is morally binding on Eliot's Executors. I am sorry if I misled you during our telephone conversation. I had temporarily forgotten the memorandum. Yours sincerely, A. R. Jabez-Smith.

1972

January 4, 1972

Another cold trail. This letter received this morning from MISS SCARTH:

> Dear Sir: Thank you for your letter but I am afraid I cannot help you very much, as I do not recall the Frenchwoman's name or whether she was there when Mr. Eliot and Mr. Hayward lived together. I do remember Mr. Eliot's first wife's death. With regrets that I have not been very helpful, Yours truly, G. H. Scarth.

January 5, 1972

Today a postcard from MRS. OAKELEY, JOHN HAYWARD's sister, saying as follows:

> Mrs. Thompson has remembered Madame's name. Is it Amery so we are getting on! (no answer required to this clue).

I sent this information on to PAT GARRATT whom I hadn't heard from for some time, asking her if she could scout around among the boarding-houses off Lotts Road and find out if there was a woman named MRS. AMERY who owned one.

January 7, 1972

Several items to add today, dear Diary. In the first place I should catch up with Christmas. and mention a Christmas card which I got from BARBIE STURTEVANT. A long delayed answer to my letter to her months ago, it says: "Bless you Tom for your rarely (she means 'really') meticulous memory! I am glad to know where I stand re VALERIE. Had a Christmas card from her – affectionate, saying nothing about anything. Guess she is just busy. No – have made no decisions. At present everything is still Houghton 'on deposit' – will have to think some more! She's referring here to the disposal of the contents of the house in Cambridge of a cousin of her and of ELIOT's. I don't remember her cousin's name but her nickname was YAYA I think. She left everything to BARBIE and her brother, HOLMES. They were deciding what to do; whether to pass the whole thing over to the Houghton Library to join the main ELIOT collection or not; they still haven't made up their minds.] My brother is unavailable at present – his life upset by violent changes, and abroad just now, and then back to Japan. His name is HOLMES H. WELCH, but he is in Europe, then back to Harvard briefly. All ELIOT letters belong to me, not my brother. Will notify you first of any 'change in policy'..." (then it goes off into personal messages).

Next I have a reply from PROFESSOR DONALD GALLUP, to my letter telling him about the errors in the Facsimile Waste Land. The letter is dated 4th January, 1972

> Dear Mr. Matthews: Thank you very much for your letter of 18th December with the enclosure. It's always difficult to know what to do about pointing out errors: you're damned if you do and damned if you don't. So far as The Waste Land Facsimile is

concerned, it seems to me that the reviewers have been impressed, and quite properly too, with the very fine job that Valerie Eliot has done in transcribing this often very difficult material, in inspiring the Oxford University Press printers to a superb printing achievement, and in tracking down some of Eliot's extremely obscure references. In this kind of work it is, I am convinced, impossible to catch all errors. The text itself, which I have been over quite carefully, seems remarkably free of error, and I think that Mrs. Eliot in concentrating on the text probably neglected to check and re-check her own editorial apparatus with equal care. I am sure there is no 'conspiracy of silence on her behalf'; the reviewers have paid most attention to the text, have appreciated an expert job of work, and have said so.

I had not myself caught all the errors you list. (I had noticed one or two that you have apparently overlooked: the omission of some words in the last sentence on page XXXII and 'elergy' for 'elegy' in the caption on page 119 for example). Some of them are serious, certainly, and it is too bad they weren't caught. I should think there might well be a reprinting of the book – and perhaps eventually the less expensive edition for scholars that some of the reviewers have hoped for – and I am glad. you have sent the list of errata to Peter Du Sautoy.

The American edition was actually manufactured in the United States – I suppose for reasons of copyright – and film of the Oxford setting was used (one frame was 'flipped' resulting in a bad error in the American edition). Apparently the cost of producing such a book in the United States is a good deal greater in the United States than in England.

With all best wishes and thanks for sending me the list, Yours sincerely, Donald Gallup.

On the same day I had a clipping sent to me by Mrs. Rich, Leila's mother. It was from the January 2 Number of Parade, a rather sensational weekly picture supplement (illustrated supplement) that is syndicated of various American newspapers. This particular one was taken from the Baltimore News American. I'll quote it:

> Q. The poet T. S. Eliot – has anything ever been written about his private life? Was he a homosexual? Was he ever married? Why can I find no biography about this great poet? – Howard Ellison, Cambridge, Mass.
> A. Dodd, Mead & Co. recently published T. S. Eliot: A Memoir, written by his close friend, Robert Sencourt. Eliot, born in St. Louis, married a British girl, Vivien, in 1915, shortly after he arrived in London. Almost from the start the marriage was a failure. It ended formally in 1932. Two years later Eliot went to live with his vicar, Eric Cheetham. That companionship lasted: six years. Eliot then became closely allied with John Hayward, a British bibliophile, in a friendship which endured twelve years. In 1957 he married. his secretary, Valerie Fletcher. He was then 68 and a semi-invalid. She was 30. Eliot asked that no biography be written of him.

This seems to me so defamatory and damaging that I think something ought to be done about it, but I don't know quite what. I thought first of getting hold of Tim Munby or Peter Du Sautoy, or possibly Valerie's solicitor whose name is Jabez Smith, and who we are supposed to be having dinner with one of these day at the Munby's. Whatever I do, I think I'll sleep on it.

January 10, 1972

I've now slept on it, and written the following letter which I may or may not send, to PETER DU SAUTOY:

Dear Mr. Du Sautoy: A friend in America has just sent me the following cutting from Parade, for January 2. Parade, as you may or may not know, is a rather vulgar Sunday supplement syndicated to a number of popular American newspapers. Its audience is large and semi-literate, of the kind that swells the majority in elections – and helps to form public opinion: 'Q. The poet T. S. Eliot – has anything ever been written about his private life? Was he a homosexual? Was he ever married? Why can I find no biography about this great poet? – Howard Ellison, Cambridge, Mass..'

A. Dodd, Mead & Co. recently published T. S. Eliot: A Memoir, written by his close friend, Robert Sencourt. Eliot, born in St. Louis, married a British girl, Vivien, in 1915, shortly after he arrived in London. Almost from the start the marriage was a failure. It ended formally in 1932. Two years later Eliot went to live with his vicar, Eric Cheetham. That companionship lasted: six years. Eliot then became closely allied with John Hayward, a British bibliophile, in a friendship which endured twelve years. In 1957 he married. his secretary, Valerie Fletcher. He was then 68 and a semi-invalid. She was 30. Eliot asked that no biography be written of him.

It seems to me a shame that the memory of a great poet and good man should with impunity be so exposed to this sort of damaging libel. But such libels are bound to continue as long as the full account of his life continues to be suppressed.

It should hardly be necessary for me to add that the publication of the original drafts of The Waste Land, which include some shockingly bad as well as some shockingly revelatory verse, can only exacerbate the damage – especially when it becomes known, as eventually it must, that the editor has suppressed Eliot's urgent plea to John Quinn that these verses should never be published. It may also be noted, eventually, that there is a certain incongruity between the faithful obedience to his wish neither to 'facilitate or countenance' a biography of him, and the ruthless disregard of his fervent plea never to publish these unworthy lines. Yours sincerely,

Yesterday Pam and I drove over to Banbury, and without much trouble located the house of the Vinogradoffs, Broughton Grange. It was a horrible rainy day. He looked vaguely familiar to me and I asked him whether by any chance he had been at New College from 1922 to 1924; he said that was exactly the time he had been there. He didn't remember me at all but we got along all right.

We stayed for lunch and everyone talked at once unfortunately. After lunch MRS. VINOGRADOFF, who reminded me very much of my cousin BETTY but looked somewhat nicer, showed me a dozen vellum-bound photograph albums which her mother had put together on the great days of Garsington Hall in the '20's. I found about eight pictures of VIVIEN four or five of which I had never seen before; none show her very clearly but they were all quite tantalising. MRS. VINOGRADOFF said I was welcome to any one of them; she thought she had negatives for them at £20 a shot. I got the idea that what she ought to do is to make a book out of the whole collection and get either Harper or Time & Life to publish it, with an introduction by her. I told her I would put that in hand.

I also got the idea of the form of an actual book about the writing of this book which is called Making a Book or The Story of a Book, in which, instead of using the notes that I've talked and had typed in Topic A, I simply reproduce an edited form of the correspondence, starting with France's letter to me in 1970, and going on from there.

January 13, 1972

Had dinner in London with the DUVIVIERS and ELLIE read my letter to her cousin, MRS. MALONE, who used to know EMILY HALE very well, and had never answered my letter. She said there was nothing in my letter she thought would offend her, but that probably her cousin had told me everything she knew about EMILY HALE.

    ELLIE preceded to tell me a few more things that I hadn't known, such as that EMILY HALE hailed from Albany, that she was on the faculty of Smith where ELLIE knew her, and taught 'spoken English' (I should have pinned her down about what on earth that was) and 'Drama thrown in' (ELLIE's quotes). She was not pretty but not a bit mousy. She'd been waiting a long time for ELLIOT's wife to die so she could marry him; and MRS. MALONE's mother, AUNT MOLLY, said, "Poor EMILY!"

    That's about what I got out of her. Then the next evening she rang up to say that EMILY HALE was not <u>certainly</u> born in Albany, but she was certainly no a Boston HALE; that she taught at Smith in ELLIE's mother's day in the 1930's. So I think what I'll have to do is to write down all that I think I know about EMILY HALE, all I've been told about her, and get ELLIE to check it) because there are too many discrepancies and gaps.

January 15, 1972

Two letters from my researcher, PAT GARRATT; one, enclosing a marvellous letter from a woman named JEANNE HESTON from Chipping Camden, who knew EMILY HALE and said what she knew about her – here's a bit of the letter:

> ...My family and I are Unitarians who came from Edgbaston to Chipping Camden in 1925 and have had a home here ever since, and we were delighted to welcome fellow Unitarians from the States, Dr. Carol Perkins, having been the Minister of the Unitarian

Chapel Royal, Boston, Massachusetts, and Miss Sunderland-Taylor.

Miss Sunderland-Taylor used to let her charming Stamford House to these three Americans for two or three months each summer while travelling on the proceeds sometimes with me and T. S. Eliot always visited the Carol Perkin's when they were in Camden.

Though Emily Hale always spoke of her two companions as Uncle and Aunt, I seem to remember her telling me she was in actual fact their ward, but this can have no bearing on your biography of the poet... [breaks off]

... Cathedral. And my sister remembers being invited to tea in the garden of Stamford House by the three friends after which Mr. Eliot read some of his poems.

Mrs. Carol Perkins was a gifted amateur photographer and keen gardener and she delighted in taking colour photographs of Cotswold gardens while she was in the district...

Were they alive now, Dr. and Mrs. Perkins would be over a hundred years old and Emily in her late seventies, but I feel in my bones [breaks off]

January 14, 1972

I heard ALEC GUINNESS on BBC 2 reading <u>Little Gidding</u> last night. It showed a picture of the church which I had seen and of the farmyard which you go through to get to it; he told a little about it and then read the poem. He spoke of the innocent unworldliness of the Ferrar community and made a few remarks about ELIOT himself:

> "I have rarely met a man who could laugh so richly and warmly; and who also liked dry Martinis, and

who was so humble..." – that I could have spared – but he did read <u>Little Gidding</u> very well; even the parts, I think, that he didn't understand, he read quite well.

January 18, 1972

Two slight rays of light: a letter from MRS. VINAGRADOFF addressing me as "Dear Tom" and saying, "May I call you this? Please call me Julian".

And the next day, a letter from DU SAUTOY in answer to mine to him which I should say is about a perceptible ten degrees warmer than our correspondence has been hitherto. I think I might even quote it:

> Dear Mr. Matthews: Thank you very much for your letter of 10th January and for taking the trouble to bring to our notice the curious question and answer that has appeared in <u>Parade</u>. I cannot say I am familiar with <u>Parade</u>, though I think I have come across it, and I wonder if you were thinking of getting some sort of correction or comment printed, if indeed they would consider that. It is not very easy to see what might be said, but I feel that you may have had something in mind. With kind regards, Yours sincerely,

Hmm!

I think now I'll write him one of my suppressed paragraphs. I'm not going to try to get a retraction out of this; why should I? I said it to him because it seems to me a shame that the memory of a great and good man should with impunity be so exposed to this sort of damaging libel. But such libels are bound to continue as long as the full account of his life continues to be suppressed, thus leaving the field to people like SENCOURT and myself.

February 7, 1972

Our first day in Venice. VICTOR and PETER came to lunch and PAM gave them clams and white wine in our flat; then we went to the Raffaelle, which is close by. Who should be there, at a table on the side, but EZRA POUND and OLGA RUDGE! My first sight of him. PETER and VICTOR stopped to speak to them. The news of death had just come, and OLGA RUDGE said to VICTOR that they wanted him to have a memorial service. When? said VICTOR. Tomorrow at 5. OLGA RUDGE also told him that there should be two hymns and told him which ones Praise the Lord, the King of Heaven; and All People that on Earth Do Dwell. VICTOR suggested that Pound should say something about MARIANNE MOORE. When she demurred, he suggested that Pound should read a poem of MARIANNE MOORE. She thought that an excellent idea. I think she also said that when VICTOR put a notice about the service in the paper, the notice should be in English. VICTOR did put such a notice in the Gazzettino, in English, and also telephoned to various people about the service. We figured that at least ten people should show up.

As well as I could during lunch I watched these two white-faced, white-haired old people from our table on the other side of the room. They seemed to talk to one another occasionally, but it was hard to be sure. Both their faces were harrowed with age; but her wrinkles seemed to express anxiety, his a kind of rapscallious indifference. Once or twice they looked in my direction, as if they felt my stare. I wanted to see how he moved as he walked, but they got away before I was aware of their going. A handsome old man, who bore little likeness to the chubby jeune homme terrible of 50 years ago, but his head is not well-shaped (did JOAN FITZGERALD cheat a little in her sculptured heads of him?); the back of his head somehow detracts from the time-sharpened nose and brow. It should be a noble head, and partly is – but something detracts from it, diminishes it.

Sixteen (18?) people came to the memorial service. VICTOR read a les son from the Bible and said several prayers, and then we sang the two hymns. Then Pound read a poem by MARIANNE MOORE – <u>The After Years</u> (1941). He read it from a large piece of cardboard, written in a flowing hand (apparently with a brush pen) on both sides. I was across the aisle and two rows back and couldn't hear a word. Pam thought she caught some phrases. On the second side, as he approached the end, he made a little gesture – a flip of his right hand – and as he came to the bottom of the page he paused for several seconds, either because he couldn't make out what he was reading or was momentarily too moved to continue. (I think it was the former.)

When the service was over we all waited till he and OLGA RUDGE went down the aisle, then we followed. There was a group by the front door inside the church. I spoke to JOAN FITZGERALD, and then VICTOR motioned to me and I shook EZRA POUND's small, bony, almost lifeless hand; then OLGA RUDGE's. So now I've met him.

February 12, 1972

Party at JOAN FITZGERALD's, where I saw her new head of Diomede and some other things. Everyone seems aware of the ELIOT project. PEGGY GUGGENHEIM asked me how it was going, and I replied at such length that she looked stunned and asked us to drinks next Wednesday!

A dinner party at Harry's Bar given by LAURANCE and ISABEL ROBERTS: 12 people, and we were the last to arrive. I was on ISABEL ROBERT's left, between her and MRS. MCANDREW; Pam was between JOHN MCANDREW and PHILIP HOFER, emeritus librarian of the Houghton Library at Harvard. The others: SIR ASHLEY and LADY CLARKE (he was formerly British ambassador at Rome), Professor and MRS. MASON HAMMOND (Ex Classics professor at Harvard, at present curator at I Tatti). The food was delicious but I didn't do it justice; talked too much.

After dinner HOFER informed me that he had a considerable correspondence between himself and ELIOT but that it was locked up for some time to come. It had happened about 1939–40, a very bad-tempered exchange (fanned by JOHN HAYWARD, who was HOFER's friend: he told each one the other disliked him extremely). This artificial quarrel was composed by the LAMB sisters (ROSAMUND and AIMEE), cousins and adorers of TSE; through their good offices ELIOT and HOFER had lunch together and agreed to bury the hatchet. ELIOT promised to write HOFER a letter saying how sorry he was about the whole affair. In that case, said HOFER, he undertook to put the whole correspondence under lock and key for a generation to come. And so it was.

January 12, 1972 From TSM to Miss Cyrilly Abels

... Yesterday PAM and I went to lunch near Banbury with the daughter of LADY OTTOLINE MORRELL (the hostess with the moistest – at least as far as the arts were concerned – of the 1920s) so that I could see her photograph albums, which included some snaps of VIVIENNE ELIOT.

It was a very pleasant and invigorating lunch, and I came away with ideas for three books (BOB CANTWELL used to say that his besetting sin was writing books at lunch). But these are serious, and I'm writing you to suggest that you give first refusal of at least two of them to Harper & Row. Here they are; I'll lead off wit the two for Harper:

> 1) Album of the '20s: pictures (blown up to generous size) of weekends of Garsington Hall, with an introduction by Mrs. Vinogradoff. Some of the cast of characters: Lytton Strachey, Katherine Mansfield, E. M. Forster, L. P. Hartley, Duncan Grant, David Garnett, Ottoline Morrell, Siegfried Sassoon, Carrington, etc., etc., etc.
>
> 2) Story of a Book: the story of my book on Eliot, told almost entirely in letters, beginning

with Frances Lindley's first letter to me and
going on from there. (The letters would of course
be edited and cut; and it might be necessary to
have some connecting stuff between some of them. I
have the raw material for this connective tissue
in the typed record I've kept – nearly 200 pages
to date.) I think the letters that tell a story
can be fascinating; the that this could be quite
interesting. . . .

From a letter dated January 22, 1972, CYRILLY ABELS to TSM

. . . What a creative lunch! Everyone of your
suggestions is enticing. I had already made a date to
see Frances for lunch yesterday, and we discussed the
first two ideas.
    She, too, thinks the suggestion of the 20's Album
sounds great[54] . . . About the second, the story of a
book, we both thought the facts would make a fine
magazine article, as you would do it (I let her say
first, because I'd made up my mind that it wasn't a
saleable book idea but that it might be an article or
a preface to the book). . . .

February 13, 1972

Met the HOFERS again at a lunch put on by the MCANDREWS at a trattoria, the Vecia Cavana (very good) near the Ca' d'Oro: and MRS. MCANDREW put HOFER next to me, so he could tell me his story over again. He did, also urged me to write MISS AIMEE LAMB and ask her help! And he gave me various other addresses that might come in handy: J. Douglas Bush, the Harvard Alumni Association, Harvard Archives; and a collector of

---

54 *Lady Ottoline's Album* was published by Knopf in 1976, edited by the US feminist literary critic Carolyn G. Heilbrun with an introduction by Lord David Cecil.

photographs, DAVIS PRATT. Some of whom I shall write to. HOFER seems anxious to help me; he also seems to me a bit of a <u>faux bonhomme</u>. Ah well.

February 14, 1972

PETER LAURITZEN tells me the following Eliotana (which may or may not be strictly true): that the photograph of TSE on the jacket of Collected Poems (PETER thinks it was about 1958) shows TSE in a suit made by Langrock, a Princeton tailor.

And that when TSE won the Nobel Prize he came into Lahiere's restaurant, where THOMAS MANN was having lunch (hadn't MANN left PRINCETON long before?); also present: ALBERT EINSTEIN, HERMANN BROCH and ERIC KAHLER (who's he?). TSE behaved like a schoolboy and KAHLER said, "What's up?" EINSTEIN replied, "Oh, he's won the Nobel Prize."

February 20, 1972

JOAN FITZGERALD came to dinner with us and told us in detail about her run-in with HOFER at Peggy Guggenheim's party. He told her the same story he told me, but with variations, and was obviously trying to justify himself, and wanted her approval and sympathy. She gave him neither, whereupon he got angry. She thinks he must be crackers. She says he still hates ELIOT, for two reasons: TSE called him "a pip-squeak," and (according to HOFER) said he was not fit to be the head of the Houghton Library and should be deprived of the job. HOFER then threatened to publish their correspondence – or sell it for $4,000; I'm not clear about this – unless ELIOT wrote him a letter of apology (which he did, HOFER says). Hofer thereupon locked up all the letters "for a hundred years." But he can't keep from talking about it.

JOAN told him he should have thrown away the whole file, and forgotten it. "What!" he cried; "destroy the evidence?"

JOAN talked a lot about Pound. She won't actually say she thinks him the best poet of the 20th century (and maybe she wouldn't put him ahead of Yeats or ELIOT) but she tried to get me to rank him – with his contemporaries and with the big boys of past days. She was pleased that I said he was better than WHITMAN. She played me part of a record from last year's Festival at Spoleto, with Pound reading part of Canto XVI. It was an old man's voice, but pretty clear, and he read it straight, without the chanting I'd been told was characteristic of him as a young man. It read well.

February 27, 1972

In today's <u>Observer</u> the following paragraphs:

> Will the T. S. Eliot biography – the one that never was and apparently never could be written – happen after all? There are hopeful whispers. Faber & Faber, Eliot's publishers, are doing some cautious talking and exploring, but it all depends on Valerie Eliot, the writer's widow and sole literary executor. So far her faithful (some would say, fierce) execution of her husband's instructions 'neither to facilitate nor countenance any biography' has been absolute.
>
> Now she is conceding that it may be necessary to find a biographer; and even to list the 'right person's' essential attributes: 'real understanding' of the American background besides a knowledge of England and Europe; sympathy with Eliot's religious outlook; 'above all ... empathy'.
>
> Valerie Eliot's hard line may have been affected by the late Robert Sencourt's recently published and savagely criticized <u>Memoir</u> of Eliot: as his publishers, Garnstone Press, are happy to point out. 'It gives her a green light to authorize a full

biography, to correct all Sencourt's errors,' they say. Literati closer to her agree that it's become a matter of which pressure she gives in to; that she may see an official biography as the only way of stopping books like Sencourt's.

And the lucky biographer? Hottest tip would seem to be Richard Ellmann, the American academic, whose biographical and critical works on Yeats and Joyce have become classics. Ellmann, who is a graduate of Yale and Trinity College, Dublin, and was English professor at Northwestern and Yale Universities, has been lying low in Oxford (as Goldsmith professor) since 1970, busily composing his long promised life of Oscar Wilde.

February 29, 1972

In Paris I saw a woman named GRETA DAVIS, recommended by BOBBY BAKER, who used to work for TIME in New York, and is now free-lancing in Paris. He recommended her as a possible researcher, so I met her, didn't particularly take to her, and perhaps she to me, but I gave her a little list of queries on ELIOT's year in Paris, and told her that the job would probably only last until the 1st June this year because by that time presumably all queries would be answered.

March 24, 1972

PAT GARRATT has hit some pay dirt. She has sent me a letter from the retired churchwarden at Chipping Camden, a MR. JOHN HORNE, who remembers EMILY HALE, and says this about her:

> Dr. Carol Perkins and his wife were regular visitors to Chipping Camden from approximately 1934 until 1939. Miss Emily Hale occupied an adjoining cottage known as Stanley Cottage. It was at this cottage

that Mr. Eliot used to stay when he visited Chipping
Camden. . . .Mr. Eliot although a frequent visitor to
Stanley Cottage made only short stays. . . .Miss Emily
Hale came back to this country several times after
the war and she usually made a short stay in Camden
during her visits to England. . . .She made a short
visit about two years ago and I had an opportunity to
talk to her. She came to the parish church for one of
the services. . . she was looking much older and said
that she expected this would be her last visit.

PAT also sent me a letter from some woman – I can't
remember her name – who got EMILY HALE mixed up with
NANCY HALE. But that reminded me of NANCY HALE whom I have
never met but one of whose husbands, CHARLES WESTENBAKER,
I used to know very well, and I looked up her address in
Who's Who. She is married to a professor at the University
of Virginia, and now I've written to her, asking if she's
by any chance any kin to Emily, or if she knows anything
about her.

I've also heard at last from V. S. PRITCHETT who I was just
despairing of. I had now written and asked him if he could
put me in touch with someone at Smith who could give me some
information about EMILY HALE, and he said that the person
he knew there on the faculty had gone to Harvard, and all
he could do was suggest that I write to the secretary of the
English department, which I have done.

March 29, 1972

A lunch in London at Buck's, with LAURIE and KATHY. Fairly
unsatisfactory. KATHY had an anecdote – so-called – about
FATHER CHEETHAM, but all it turned out to be was that he
loved dress-making, and had a young pal called Peter who was
rather a good singer. And once, VICTORIA's grand-daughter,
PRINCESS MARIE LOUISE, one of his parishioners, who was

organising a concert, went to see FATHER CHEETHAM and he was trying on some women's clothes which he had designed and made.

Then LAURIE told me some cock-and-bull story about the only time he'd ever seen ELIOT was at lunch with various other notables – GORONWY REES and so on – and the waitress had spilled some soup with croutons in ELIOT's lap who took it very well; he simply brushed himself off, and when the waitress said she hoped he was all right, he said, according to LAURIE, "Oh yes, I've just salvaged three."

I said to LAURIE, "That's absolutely impossible because he pronounces it as if it were <u>Salváges</u>." "Oh well, you know me!" said LAURIE.

I'm really pretty fed-up with that.

March 30, 1972

Had lunch at the same place with VERA RUSSELL, ex-wife of several people, the last one JOHN RUSSELL, the art critic. A Russian lady who claimed to have been the guiding light, or one of the guiding lights in the Group Theatre which started around 1932, went on until the War, then started again in '48 and finally died in '54.

She says that there is an E.M.I. record of the <u>Sweeney</u> show as performed at the memorial show that she put on; I must try to get it.

The Group Theatre started on Great Newport Street, next to the Arts Theatre, then moved to Goodwin's Court, and also produced in other theatres. The man who ran it, according to Vera, was RUPERT DOON, who started off life as one of Diaghileff's boys, apparently.

She said that VIVIEN used to come. She couldn't tell me much about her but she says that a woman named CONSTANCE FOULJAMBES, daughter of the Duke of Manchester, knew VIVIEN well, and I should see MRS. (?) FOULJAMBES.

She also says that I should hear the BBC memorial programme on the 3rd in memory of PAUL VALERY, she thinks about 1949, text written by JOHN HAYWARD and TSE contributed.

She was full of big names of people I ought to see: SIR HENRY AVIGDOR GOLDSMID, D.S.O., M.C., 10 Eaton Mansions, Sloane Square; he was one of several people., according to VERA RUSSELL, who financed JOHN HAYWARD; another was VICTOR ROTHSCHILD; and one was LORD ROTHERMERE, whom I should see about his mother's papers, to see if she has something about the <u>Criterion</u>. I should know her – she back ELIOT in the <u>Criterion</u> originally.

Then also CECIL KING, she said I should see. He lives at Hampton Court, she thinks.

I should ask TIM MUNBY if there isn't a letter in the HAYWARD papers from ELIOT to HAYWARD – thus proving there was a letter apropos his leaving HAYWARD.

And I certainly should see. JOHN CARTER at Sotheby's, she said, who was a great friend of HAYWARD.

She said she knew HAYWARD very, very well, and also claims to have known ELIOT very, very well. Of ELIOT she said: "He was hard. Kindly? I don't think so. And he could be <u>very</u> angry."

March 31, 1972

Last night I dreamed that ELIOT was staying with us. He was lean, lank, affable, very willing to answer all my questions – I could think of very few – and I was writing a cover story, as I usually do in one of these worry dreams; I was writing a cover story about him.

At one point I said, "I'm glad I didn't know you when you were young," meaning that he would have been too brilliant, and perhaps too unkind.

He understood all right. "Yes," said he. "I've got better and better; now I'm as good as <u>I can</u> be."

April 8, 1972

This is a day I've been waiting for, for pretty close to two years I suppose. Here it is at last, and I wish it were over. MAURICE HAIGH-WOOD is coming for the night and the rest of the weekend, and, presumably, will talk to me and answer my questions; but I don't believe he has any answers whatever.

Later:
Here are the fruits of two hours' general conversation. He and his late wife lived four to five years in the south of Spain, near Marbella but two or three kilometers inland, in the hills. They didn't live there all the time, they went away in the summer. At the same time, they had a house in the Algarve which he mostly let.

After he gave up Spain, I gather he went to live in Portugal. He used to speak both Spanish and Portuguese, but has lost them; he still speaks Italian though.

April 9, 1972

Perhaps pessimism has paid off again. I've just had an hour-an hour-and-a-half's go with MAURICE HAIGH-WOOD, and he's a good man; a good grey man but a good man. Let's see if I can remember part of it.

His father was a sort of child prodigy painter, apparently, who then developed a knack of painting portraits, and, for a while, painted portraits and genre pictures (pictures that told a story) seriously, to make money. Then, apparently, he inherited some money and made it quite unnecessary for him to go on earning any, so he and his wife used to travel a great deal, but he still took his sketch book along. He no longer depended upon portrait-painting for his money.

Alas, he painted portraits of his wife, MAURICE, his son, and VIVIEN[55], his daughter, all of which were destroyed by

---

55 Vivien Eliot spelled her name two ways. This manuscript preserves the way Matthews spelled it.

enemy action in (I think he said) the PETER JONES depository in London.

The HAIGH-WOODs lived in Hampstead in-house in Compayne Gardens; VIVIEN and MAURICE were the only children. VIVIEN was eight years older than MAURICE; she went to the King Alfred School till she was about fourteen, then to a boarding school at Eastbourne – her brother can't remember the name – he says Eastbourne is stiff with girls' boarding schools; that was apparently the extent of her education.

She was very attractive to boys and had lots of beaux. One man was so cut-up about being turned down when he proposed marriage to her that he walked from one end of London to the other, all night long, trying to get over it.

Her hair was not black, but very dark brown; her eyes, he thinks, were blue-grey.

As a child of about seven or eight, she had tuberculosis of the hand and was operated on (I never heard of this kind of thing), and was sent to MARGATE[56] with her mother for a long spell, to recover. Her nerves were so on edge by all this, and her hearing so sensitive, that she thought she couldn't stand anybody laughing loudly. If she saw someone in her presence who she thought was about to laugh, she'd say, "Don't let him laugh!"

I learned from her brother how VIVIEN & ELIOT met. She and ELIOT did not meet in any romantic way in neighboring punts, as SACHEVERELL SITWELL[57] said, but they met through SCOFIELD THAYER,[58] a rich American who had been at school with ELIOT and was an undergraduate at Magdalen when TSE was also at Oxford and later became publisher of *The Dial*,

---

56 A seaside resort where Eliot later traveled with Vivien and, notably, wrote a section of *The Waste Land*.
57 Sir Sacheverell Reresby Sitwell (1897–1988) was an English art and music critic, and the younger brother of Dame Edith Sitwell and Sir Osbert Sitwell.
58 Scofield Thayer (1889–1982), wealthy art collector and owner of *The Dial*.

whose cousin, LUCY THAYER, had met the HAIGH-WOODs in Switzerland, at Christmas 1908.

Another man named THWING, although an American, was at Sandhurst with MAURICE HAIGH-WOOD, he says. He went to Sandhurst for an apparently shortened course during the War, was immediately gazetted to the Manchester Regiment, and went out to France and was wounded there.

I went through my list of questions. I can't see any examples of his father's paintings because they're all scattered around among the people who bought them as portraits.

His family came from Bury, in Lancashire? No, no. Anyway, they lived in Hampstead.

VIVIEN changed her name from VIVIENNE to VIVIEN some time after she married; he doesn't know why. He has no photographs of her. She was a very good ballroom dancer and at one point, as a fad, took up ballet dancing with a friend, but didn't get very far with it, she just studied it a bit.

He indignantly denies that she was an ether drinker, says that naturally she was given drugs at her hospital, for her illnesses, but she was never an addict.

Alas, the myth that ELIOT visited her in the hospital once a week, or once a month, as long as she lived, is not true, he says. He never did see her again – VALERIE's right about that – he never saw her again after 1932, and he did break the news to her that he wasn't coming back by sending a letter through his lawyer.

Her mental condition, her brother describes as not <u>non compos mentis</u>, but as of temperamental and a form of obstinacy. He cited as an instance of this, her Will, in which she left some property in Ireland to her nephew, his son, which she knew perfectly well had been sold, but she just didn't want to admit that it had been sold, so she left it, of course, quite illegally.

He raises an eyebrow about the story that SENCOURT[59] tells on page 137, that she showed up at a lecture or reading of ELIOT's.

VIVIEN was never certified. She may have been continuously in hospital for the last years of her life, but although it was a mental hospital she was not certified as insane.

HAIGH-WOOD says that he and his sister often danced together; she was a beautiful ballroom dancer, although he was too tall for her; he's well over six feet and she was below medium height.

That's the end, unless I can remember something more.

He took her writing rather lightly, and was not as enthusiastic about it as I was. I showed him the passage which I think is a description of ELIOT, and he raised an eyebrow at that too. He thought, if it was a description, it was very exaggerated. I think it was an extremely clever caricature.

HAIGH-WOOD says there's a description of VIVIEN in a book by BRIGIT PATMORE, edited by her son, DEREK PATMORE. He says also that BRIGIT PATMORE and various other people were very keen on ELIOT – mad about him, in fact, and that VIVIEN knew this and rather laughed about it.

---

59 Robert Sencourt (1890–1969), previously known as Gordon George, was a friend of Eliot's whose book, *T. S. Eliot, A Memoir,* was published posthumously, edited by Donald Adamson, in 1971. The Sencourt memoir was controversial because of its suggestion that Eliot was a homosexual. On August 25, 1931 TSE wrote to Emily Hale: "Did I ever answer your enquiry about the man you met with us? His name is Robert Esmonde Gordon George — a New Zealander — ex-officer in the Bengal Lancers — sent up to Oxford late, after the war — Roman Catholic convert, and very devout — always buzzing about with Cardinals and Abbots — lives in Hyeres, having poor health — and seems to know an immense number of people everywhere — writes under the name of Robert Sencourt — I believe his recent Life of the Empress Eugenie was very successful both here and in America. He is inclined to take a little too much upon himself, but otherwise is a very refined and sensitive person, and I like his company. Very eager interest in human beings."

He says that EDIT SITWELL was quite 'miffed' when ELIOT married VALERIE without consulting her. He thinks that one of the people who was mad about ELIOT was Mary HUTCHINSON. He didn't know about Mary Trevelyan; he's never heard of EMILY HALE.

I'm sure I've left out a lot of what he said, but that's about all I can remember at the moment.

Oh yes, the wedding was a surprise to the HAIGH-WOOD parents as well as to the ELIOTs. They knew ELIOT and liked him, but all of a sudden they got a telegram from VIVIEN, just saying, "We're married." One of the witnesses, I think, was Lucy Thayer. Though it was a surprise to their parents they soon got over it.

I think I may have struck a little pay dirt: a newspaper report of a lecture ELIOT gave at the University of Minnesota on May 1, 1956. ELIOT had made a pencilled note on it; this text is evidently that of the tape recording, and the interesting parts of the lecture are as follow:

> I do not suggest that the personality and the private life of a dead poet constitutes sacred ground on which the psychologist must not tread. The scientist must be at liberty to study such material as his curiosity leads him to investigate, as long as the victim is dead and the laws of libel cannot be invoked to stop him. Nor is there any reason why biographies of poets should not be written. They are very useful. Any critic seriously concerned with a man's work should be expected to know something about the man's life. The question of how far information about the poet helps us to understand the poetry is not so simple as one might think. Each reader must answer it for himself, and in particular instances, for it may be more important in the case of one poet, and less important in the case of another.

Now why do you suppose ELIOT changed his mind? Some time in the next nine years, which was as much as he had to live, he evidently did change his mind. When he made this lecture at the University of Minnesota in 1956 he had not yet married VALERIE.

DR. MUNBY told me today that he had lately seen MRS. ELIOT's lawyer who, it appears is a very old chum of his; they were at school together, and in the same regiment in the Army. He said that MRS. ELIOT, he though, might be – I can't remember the word he used – softening? relaxing? – anyway, changing her position somewhat. I said I supposed that might mean that she would appoint an official biographer—an Englishman, of course. He said, yes, he thought that might be it. I told him about my writing to her, not altogether ingenuously, in order to see whether I could get an answer out of her. And, "Did she answer" he said. I said, "No, she fell and broke her arm rather than reply."

April 10, 1972

This morning, at breakfast, I asked HAIGH-WOOD whether he could tell me what ELIOT had for breakfast, coffee or tea; I said I knew he preferred claret to burgundy, and gin to whisky. He looked a little puzzled and said it was probably coffee, but he didn't know.

Well, I got something out of him, and for what I did I should be grateful.

April 13, 1972

Letter from TIM MUNBY,[60] dated 11th April:

> Dear Tom: I found your kind letter on my return from Turkey where we have been for a fortnight.

---

60 Matthews acknowledged the help of Dr. A. N. L. Munby, librarian of King's College, Cambridge, in accessing the papers of Eliot's longtime roommate, John Hayward, that were not restricted by Hayward's will or Mrs. Eliot.

We would much have liked to have come to lunch on the 16th, but we have a houseful ourselves that weekend and have arranged a party for our visitors. I would like to see you soon, if only to report on my hour-and-a-half's tête-à-tête with Valerie. Yours ever, Tim.

April 14, 1972

A tantalizing letter from NANCY HALE, now MRS. FREDSON BOWERS, to whom I wrote a couple of weeks ago, addressing her in Charlottesville, where her husband is a professor at the University of Virginia, asking her if she could tell me anything, by any chance, about EMILY HALE; and, by gum, she can. It's a very friendly letter, which I won't quote, but she's in London, will be there until the 19th April, then they're going to Oxford where her husband is a visiting Fellow of All Souls until the middle of June; so I shall certainly make every effort to see her. She sounds very willing to tell me everything she knows which she says, alas, is not specific, but she did know EMILY HALE, and can probably remember more about her if she tries.

> I told Mr. Frank Holland, out Town Clerk, I was writing to you personally, as I am going abroad next Sunday until the middle of February, but I know he will be writing to you when he has collected some scraps of information which may be of use to you. I doubt if anyone still living in Camden knew these three people as well as we did.

PAT GARRATT also wrote me that she's on the trail of the round or catch, "<u>Great Tom</u> is Cast", and she's tracked down a folk song professor who has told her where to find it in his book; she's going to give me some stuff later.

April 17, 1972

Went to London and had lunch at Buck's with MISS MARY TREVELYAN who was still looking very much like MICHAEL HORDERN, and was the same jolly woman that I remembered. She was obviously disappointed that Pam wasn't there too.

I had a list of questions to ask her, but simply couldn't bring myself to ask her anything. Instead I got her news, which is that she is off to America about the 1st May, on a trip which will take her to various places; she starts in Atlanta, and goes as far as Berkeley, California, then back to New York. She's a little depressed about having a book she's just written, turned down; she feels that she's out of things. She has finally brought herself, apparently, to meet VALERIE, and although she speaks guardedly of her, did speak agreeably. I don't know whether she's planning to become friends, or not. As for her own reminiscence of ELIOT, which must not be mentioned, they are still in Helen Gardner's hands and I imagine they are something of a problem, for apparently they contain a good many letters from ELIOT, which, of course, VALERIE would have to give her permission to print, and that's one of the hold-ups.

We parted with expressions of mutual esteem, and I said that I might send her a list of questions.

Later in the afternoon, about 4 o'clock, I went around to the Whitehall Hotel in Montague Street, to meet MRS. FREDSON BOWERS, née NANCY HALE, once married to CHARLES WERTENBAKER, and the short story writer. She was a very handsome lady, such as I had imagined she would be, and was terribly agreeable. She have me tea; I showed her what I had about EMILY HALE, and she was very sympathetic, and as helpful as she could be. She gave me the names of several ladies in Massachusetts; Smith, who knew ELIOT well; I'm a little confused about this as I think most of them just knew ELIOT, but one or two of them knew Emily as well.

I told her that we would certainly meet again, and I was going to send her a list of questions if I could think of something specific that she might be able to help me with. And that was about the end of it.

April 20, 1972

JOHN NICOLL, the son of my old friend STEWART NICOLL, spent the night here last night. He works for the Clarendon Press at Oxford, and was very much interested in my story about VIVIEN's papers at the Bodleian, and the impossibility of getting them out, and the fact that the Bodleian's deputy curator said that they made their own rules. He thinks that, I should try to raise hell about it in the precincts of the Times Literary Supplement, in some such stages as follows: to go and see Shackleton, the Librarian of the Bodleian; get him to admit that, in effect, the Bodleian makes its own rules, therefore refusing to give me access to the papers; then I would ask him to put it in writing, and when I have his letter, lay it out in a letter to the Editor of the Times Literary Supplement.

I then suggested that I might add another step to that. (Oh, he says that he has a friend on the Times Literary Supplement that he might tip off in advance in case they might want to do something in their commentary besides the letters column.) And I thought I might go and see Bernard Levin, lay the whole thing out for him, and see if he would write a column or so about it in The Times.

Anyway, the first step, apparently, is to see SHACKLETON, who, JOHN agrees, is completely in the pocket of HELEN GARDNER, who is also on the board of the Bodleian. Anyway, I have now written a letter to SHACKLETON which I haven't posted yet, asking him if he'll let me come and see him on Tuesday, 6th June.

April 21, 1972

Thinking over my talk with JOHN NICOLL, I decided to try writing SHACKLETON, the Bodleian Librarian, a letter that would be designed, at least, to cut out the necessity of going down to Oxford and see him, and then have another letter between us, and so on – cut the whole thing down to one. So I wrote him a letter that was supposed to do that, telling him about my precious turndown by the Bodleian, and quoting some of a letter that COLIN OLIVER had drafted for me to send to the University of Texas, and also the Houghton Library at Harvard, asking by what right they forbade me access to their papers.

This is a slightly different case because the questions of copyright, I don't think, arises. Anyway, the Bodleian is supposed to be the sole owner of the VIVIEN ELIOT papers, and they don't belong to VALERIE. Well, we'll see what happens.

I've sent the letter to JOHN NICOLL and asked him to send it on to SHACKLETON _if_ he thinks well of it; if he doesn't, to send it back to me with his suggestions.

April 26, 1972

Lunch with ALAN MCLEAN of Macmillan who wanted to know what stage I had reached in the ELIOT project, and after I had told him, he suggested that I send him a copy of the outline and draft of the blurb that I was sending to FRANCES LINDLEY, and that he would present them to his superior, and he thought then that Macmillan would give me a contract for the book.

I said that was all right, I thought, but I would prefer to have Frances see that stuff first, and see if she had any objection to it. So I promised to send her off the stuff the next day.

April 27, 1972

I typed out the little, sub-title, outline of chapter heads, and the time span each chapter covered, the places of each chapter and ELIOT's ages, also the rough draft of the blurb; I then sent them off to Frances, telling her about my lunch with Alan McLean.

April 30, 1972

The MUNBYs came to lunch, and afterwards TIM MUNBY gave me a report of his hour-and-a-half tête-à-tête with VALERIE. He told me what he had told her, and he said, "You know you're not her favourite man." And why? Because I'd sent in all these lists of editorial mistakes that she had made in these two different books.

But he told her that she ought to read <u>Name and Address</u>, that my background was very similar to ELIOT's, that I was just the man to write a book on ELIOT's youth in America. Whereupon, she said, according to him: "I wish he would do that."

He suggested that he would write and tell VALERIE that he had seen me and talked to me about this, and that I had been, at least, interested.

He said that this might lead to a meeting between me and VALERIE at least, and that we might even come to some sort of agreement by which I could then, presumably, have access to papers that covered his youth – whatever that date would stop at – and also get permission to quote.

I said I would certainly think about it; so that's what he's going to do, write to her, and then I'll wait and hear either from him, of from VALERIE.

May 1, 1972

Lunch in London with JOHN CARTER, old friend of JOHN HAYWARD's, now a big shot in Sotheby's; a very lean, silvery, personably, old Etonian, who looks rather like a very valuable silver spoon.

We had a very nice lunch, but I don't think I got anything at all out of him.

TIM MUNBY sent me a copy of the letter he had written to VALERIE in which he says <u>she</u> may be hearing from <u>me</u>; so I've written to him saying that wasn't the way I understood it, but I'm perfectly willing – Barks is willing but Peggoty's got to make some sort of sign. So I'm going to wait until I hear from him, or directly from her; but he's to let me know what her reaction was to the letter.

May 7, 1972

The VINOGRADOFFS were here for the weekend, and today I went over the photograph albums that she had brought with her, and picked out the two photographs of VIVIEN taken at Garsington, about 1916 or 1916, that I want. JULIEN is going to find the negatives if she can and send them to me, and then I'll get them blown up. I think one will be enough, but I've got two just in case.

I also had a talk with her about TS and VIVIEN, and got these replies from her:

She was nine when she first met the ELIOTs, and altogether saw them, I suppose, about three times, always at Garsington Manor.

I asked her what was her impression of TS, and she said he was tall, friendly and strikingly good-looking.

She told me a story about a dinner or lunch one day, when DUNCAN GRANT, asked what he thought about somebody's pictures, said: "Very interesting." ELIOT leaned over the table and said: "And what, precisely, do you mean by 'very interesting'?" This raised a laugh, and became a sort of family expression: "And what, precisely, do you mean. . .?"

Her impressions of VIVIEN were that she was – "actressy" was the word she used, and "coy", "flirtatious", "amusing", "not clever", "quick on the uptake", "vivacious".

JULIEN thought that VIVIEN was, perhaps, fonder of ELIOT than he was of her.

I said: "Would you say that ELIOT was really kind and modest, and arrogant and holding himself in?" And she thought that he was not modest – how could he be? – but he was kind.

She learned <u>Prufrock</u> by heart, at the age of ten, and was once called on by her mother to recite it to Virginia Woolf.

She liked all his property, and never stopped liking it. She went on beyond <u>Ash Wednesday</u>.

She said there was a lot of talk about VIVIEN, and particularly from Maria Huxley who, she said, was rather a malicious person, saying that VIVIEN always smelled of ether, and there were stories that she was a drug addict.

She also told me about some letters from ELIOT to her mother which she had sold to the University of Texas, I believe. She said they were very affecting, quite emotional, mainly about VIVIEN and her illness, and their difficulties.

May 11, 1972

A letter this morning from MR. STANLEY BARRON of Thames & Hudson, asking if there is any chance of his firm being allowed to publish my book on ELIOT.

So I wrote back, telling him what the situation was, and that he was now the sixth (I think) London publisher to enquire about it; that Macmillan have an option and they are mulling it over about whether or not to give me a contract; that if he likes to enquire from MR. ALAN MCLEAN whether or not they're going to give me a contract, if he can. If Macmillan's decide not to, I said I'd of course be interested in some other publisher; that might make Macmillan's make up their minds.

May 12, 1972

I had a letter from JULIEN VINOGRADOFF who told me she has been unable to find the negatives of the two photographs of VIVIEN, at Garsington, which I had chosen from her mother's photograph album when the VINOGRADOFFS were here last weekend. She is trusting me with the page so I am going to take it to WALLACE HEATON and get the pictures reproduced somehow.

I typed out an agreement between us, which I'll read:

May 7, 1972. This will serve as a reminder to both Julien and Tom of the details of the arrangement they have agreed on, under which Tom is to use one, or possibly two of Julien's photographs of Vivien Eliot for his book.

Julien will find the negatives (if she can) of both the photographs Tom wants and send them to him; he will have blown-up copies made and return the negatives to her. Tom has paid Julien twenty pounds for the use of one picture and if he uses the other in his book he will pay a further twenty pounds.

Tom's use of one or both pictures in his book does not preclude Julien's use of both of them in her proposed picture book about Garsington Hall.

The only other thing to add today, May 12th, is that there is still now word from SHACKLETON. I'm going to write to JOHN NICOLL today and ask him if he can find out what is the trouble.

May 20, 1972

The following letter received this morning from (apparently his correct title) Bodley's Librarian, ROBERT SHACKLETON:

Dear Mr. Matthews: I am very sorry that it has taken so long to reply to your letter of 28 April and that even now this reply is not decisive. The truth is that the investigation of the exact conditions is taking some time; but I hope to reply to you firmly very soon. Yours sincerely, (Signed) Robert Shackleton Bodley's Librarian

May 24, 1972

Dear Diary, this will have to be put down as one of your good days. I got the following letter this afternoon, from Bodley's Librarian, ROBERT SHACKLETON:

> Dear Mr. Matthews: I am glad to say that the papers of Mrs. Vivien Eliot will be available for you for consultation on request in this library provided that you give a written undertaking not to quote from them or to use them for the purpose of any work of fiction. The other conditions relating to alteration, erasure, and addition to them apply of course automatically to any Bodleian holdings.
>   I have looked at the papers myself and do not think that you will find them of great interest. Yours sincerely, (Signed) Robert Shackleton Bodley's Librarian

And that I regard as a great moral victory, if not a break in the luck.

June 1, 1972 – D-Day

I have now heard from SHACKLETON, Bodley's Librarian, that it will be quite convenient for me to appear at his office, at 2.30 in the afternoon on June 6th, and I will then be shown the VIVIEN papers.
    This is D-Day, and this should mark the end of Topic A, and the beginning of writing the book. So, although I'm sure it is not a closed chapter, let's say – Here endeth Topic A!

ADDITION TO TOPIC A

I must report having been to Oxford, where I didn't see MR. SHACKLETON, but was allowed to have a go at VIVIENNE ELIOT's papers. There were seven packages of which I have seen the contents of one. The first one I saw had four diaries for the years 1914, 1919, 1934 and 1935. I have looked through, and taken notes on, all but the 1935 one, and I have looked through that sufficiently to find two entries which completely contradict VALERIE's statement that ELIOT and VIVIENNE never met after 1932. VIVIENNE may have been making it up out of whole cloth but it rings fairly true. She speaks of going to a lecture some time in 1935 in a London hall – I think she gives the name of the hall – and turning as she went in, and suddenly seeing him right behind her. He put his hand out and said in a very loud voice, "How do you do!" Then, after the lecture was over, which she said was excellent, she let her little dog, Polly, loose, and Polly pranced up to ELIOT and jumped at him. He paid no attention; then VIVIENNE went up to him and said, in a low voice, "Tom, when are you coming home?, and he said, "I can talk to you about it now."

That may, as I say, have been a figment of her imagination, but if it wasn't, it pretty well blows VALERIE's story.

Well, I spent two days, and got 21 pages of notes out of those three diaries, and I expect to go back on 17th July.

Yesterday, or the day before, I got a letter from TIM MUNBY putting a stop to any further chances of meeting VALERIE. He wrote this letter on 8th June:

> Dear Tom: Here is a polite but firmly unrelenting extract from a letter from Valerie of 1 June. 'I appreciate your good will in attempting to find some middle path with T. S. Matthews. Even if he does change his approach, however, I am afraid he will still have to manage without my co-operation, like any other biographer. Herbert Howarth gave quite a sound sketch

of my husband's family background in Notes on Some Figures Behind T. S. Eliot, and this he did unaided in TSE's lifetime.' Sorry my little attempt to do a Whitelaw has failed, but of course his task is easier.

As a keen amateur copyright lawyer I shall follow with interest the 'fair dealing' negotiations between your publisher and Fabers if you would do me the kindness of letting me know how they go in due course. Yours ever, Tim.

June 20, 1972

A few days ago I realised that it had been more than a month since I had sent my so-called 'outline' and chapter headings to ALAN MACLEAN, on the strength of which he was going to give me some kind of answer on behalf of his firm, Macmillan – either a contract or not. So I simply sent him a one-line note saying, "Remember me?" and I got this reply very promptly, 16th June:

> Dear Tom: Thank you for the reminder which I well deserved. I went away for a holiday and still haven't really caught up. I am very much aware that when we were lunching I said I would be glad to give you 'an official yea or nay' on the book on the basis of a synopsis, etc. and, while I am happy to tell you 'officially' that we would like to publish the book when it is written, I am frankly still at a loss to judge the size of the sales potential at this end. Ideally, from the publishers' point of view, I think it is probably a book which should have joint Anglo-American production, i.e., we both draw from the same printing. But this, of course, might not be agreeable to Harpers. My guess at this stage is that our sales would be in the neighbourhood of 2,000 copies, but it could be less if those who are hostile to your book organise themselves effectively. I would be quite

willing to make a contract with you because I have
no doubt that your book will be good in itself, and
as good as it is possible to make a book when so many
primary sources are denied to you. But I don't think
at this stage I would be justified in making more than
a rather measly offer. This I would naturally make to
your agent. If you and she feel, as you well may, that
your British publisher should stick his neck out a bit
further, then I would not of course want to try to stop
you accepting a better offer from another publisher.

I am afraid this all sounds rather gloomy and
defensive, but the truth is, that in spite of your
admirable draft blurb which sets out the lines of
the book very clearly, the book itself remains to be
written, and the strength of the opposition at the
time of publication, unguessable. The best therefore
that I can do is to say – yes, please, we would like to
publish, and I will happily make an offer now, but it
won't be a sizeable one.

With best wishes and renewed apologies for the
delay, Yours ever, Alan.

I sent a copy of this letter to FRANCES LINDLEY, and also
another to CYRILLY ABELS, my New York agent, and asked for
their advice.

September 2, 1972

Notes of a conversation with MARY TREVELYAN at Cavendish Hall:

What about M. T. herself? Pam thinks she may be wacky. I am reasonably sure she is a most unreliable witness. Item: her positive statement that JOHN HAYWARD never said one word against ELIOT after being cruelly abandoned. On the other hand, when she says TSE was a great walker-away from unpleasant facts she is more credible.

I think TSE was a very sensitive and complicated person whose "friends" were less complicated – and less fundamentally tough.

M. T. kept a Journal of her friendship with TSE, starting about 1939 and ending with his second marriage in 1957. It contains more than 100 letters from TSE to her – long and funny, some of them. The original draft of this Journal, she says, is "unprintable" (I suppose because it is too intimate?). [Handwritten note added: No – because it says too many hurting things about people still alive.] She showed an edited version first to HELEN GARDNER, then to VALERIE ELIOT – who, after much thought and even praying about it, told M. T. she was against any more books on TSE "just at present"; that a certain amount of time should pass to let nasty rumors (about TSE being a homo and a hypochondriac) die down. (M. T. says he did in fact become "a hypochondriacal old gentleman.")

M. T. is now working on a third draft of the Journal from which TSE's sharp remarks about living people will be excised. She intends to show this to VALERIE, some months from now, and hopes to get her nihil obstat then. (She also said that, although she is not supposed to see me, she will let me read the Journal – she didn't say which version – if I would come to London and read it in her flat. And presumably take no notes. I said I would give anything to have a look at it. It was left that I am to write her at the end of September, when she returns to London from the north, and then we shall see what we shall see.

M. T. says she and TSE were very good friends – she thinks she and HAYWARD were perhaps the only real friends he had – but "I didn't love him and he didn't love me." No question of marriage – although she thinks it might not have worked out so badly. But "he was unmarriageable" (after he became "grand"): selfish, hypochondriacal ("and death – well, that's all through his poems"), couldn't take criticism. For one who was as fond of him as she says she was, this is pretty strong stuff.

She knew about EMILY HALE (but how much?) and says he dreaded his last meeting with her. It was news to her, which perhaps I shouldn't have given her, that Emily stashed more than 1,000 TSE letters in the Princeton University Library.

She knew the MIRRLEES (mother and daughter) in whose house near Guildford (Shamley Green) TSE spent part of every week during the war. M. T. was I Germany with the British Army, and remembers his amused and amusing letters about the MIRRLEES and what figures of fun they were.

Private and Confidential
Notes on a talk with T. S. M. on 2nd. September 1972.

I first met TSE in the summer of 1938 and had the privilege of a close friendship with him for nearly twenty years. In Bloomsbury his office at Faber's and my office in the University made us near neighbours and, on Chelsea Embankment our respective flats were only ten minutes walk from each other. Tom was Churchwarden at St. Stephen's Church Gloucester Road – which was my church from my early years – and my car was often in weekly use taking us to services.

During the writing of "The Cocktail Party" and "The Confidential Clerk" we had constant discussions and I was present at all the early rehearsals, as well as the first performances of these plays.

Tom was an inveterate letter-writer In the war, while I was in Brussels running a Leave Hostel for front line troops and, later, working for UNESCO in Paris, we kept up a constant correspondence, as in later years, when Tom was away from England. More than 100 of these letters have been preserved.

Our friendship was always platonic – neither of us would have had it other wise.

Mary Trevelyan C. B. E.
September 1972

November 28, 1972

After reading MARY TREVELYAN's Journal. If this doesn't actually add a new dimension to TSE, it does flesh out his somewhat skeletal figure; it makes him roundly human. I told her: "You certainly brought out the Pepys in him!" but what I should have said was not Pepys but Lear – EDWARD, not Kind. And she couldn't have been the only one in the world that had this effect on him; but her Journal is the only evidence I seen that this side of him existed – and was a constant side of him. His letters to her prattle: they're also clever and funny and easy. I told her I would proceed to forget everything I'd read – but how can I? That anecdote about the velocipede and the frilly-shirted little boy from next door who wanted to ride it and said his mother had told him he might if he let Tom blow his whistle! And ELIOT's comment, whose exact wording I have alas forgotten.

I saw LIONEL TRILLING in Oxford the next day and tried to enlist his interest and promise to do something; but as I feared he felt bound by his friendship to VALERIE, and said he thought he would have to say no. I am sure, however, that MARY should stick to her guns and reference to let VALERIE cannibalize her Journal to piece out TSE's selection of letters. TRILLING agreed with me that this would be too bad; he said he like reading a book of letters from one person. The Journal should be brought out by itself – but I can't see VALERIE ever giving her permission to publish; so I fear MARY's only recourse is to do as she has threatened, and consign the whole thing to the archives of the Oxford Press, to be exhumed after we are all in the grave.

Anyway, the effect on me of having skimmed this Journal is to throw me into the furthest and deepest confusion yet about what sort of person TSE was. In spite of all the contrary evidence (which he almost helped to pile up) he was or could be a funny, relaxed, cozy man – when he was with someone he both liked and trusted. That may have been only a rare occasion; but I wonder if it was.

I've come to another "conclusion" about Mary: that she's a gent.

AFTERWORD

By Karen Christensen

In June 1972, T. S. Matthews decided that he had enough information to begin writing *Great Tom,* and he stopped keeping the journal that comprises most of this volume. He continued to add notes to the file, including those about his meetings with Mary Trevelyan. The Princeton archive also contains many files of letters and notes from the months after he stopped keeping a journal and was focused on completing his manuscript. In fact, several key sources materialized at this late stage, among them Dorothy Elsmith, a friend of Emily Hale's.

Matthews turned in the manuscript for *Great Tom* early in 1973 and the US edition was published later that year. A UK edition appeared in 1974. The reviews were harsh, as Matthews makes clear in his introduction to this book, and sales were disappointing. *Great Tom* was, nonetheless, widely reviewed. Selections were serialized in *Esquire* and in *Vogue*, which chose to run part of the chapter on Emily Hale, with this introduction: "One of the most tantalizingly shadowed portions in the life of T. S. Eliot was his intensive friendship with an unusual woman, known since his youth, valued through his long career."

In January 1973, while Matthews was finishing his unauthorized biography, his agent in New York, Cyrilly Abels, wrote to him about continued reports of an authorized biography:

> You may already know from Edel[61] himself about this project. Bob Giroux told me about it when I lunched with him the first week I was back at my office. (By the way, I did not bring up your name to Bob--and he didn't bring it up to me either ... although he looked over my client list right at the table).
>
> I suppose this means that he would not undertake the T. S. Eliot biography. I did say to Bob that I had heard from the Snows (as I did) that Edel was going to undertake the book about T. S. Eliot. Bob just said that he knew Valerie was considering him among others but had not, as far as he knew, come to any decision.
>
> When I was dining with Howard Newby (P. H. Newby), I had mentioned to him that I had heard Edel had been chosen to do the Eliot and he, like Bob, said he had understood that Edel was one of the names Valerie was considering. I mentioned your book to Howard. He clearly hadn't heard about it and when I realized that he knew Valerie (in part, I suppose, because of the BBC and because he is published by Faber & Faber), I quickly told him that Valerie knew about your book although she had not seen you. I also told him that although I hadn't read any chapters of the book, I knew you and your writing well enough to expect a very good one. Both Bob and Howard said what a good job Valerie had done on The Waste Land publication! I did not pass along your comments on the subject.

---

61 Leon Edel (1907–1997), a biographer whose writing on Henry James won a Pulitzer Prize and a National Book Award.

On May 14, 1973 he wrote to Frances Lindley about a few last sources, and more refusals ("Hope Mirrlees 'will not see Mr. Matthews.'"), and told her that the manuscript had been finished:

> I came to the end of the line several days ago. Chapter 9 (the last) is now at the typist's and will be returned to me in time for Christopher Sykes to read the whole thing next weekend; he's coming here then, with that in mind.
> The last two chapters are still far from finished, and will have to be operated on. Also inserts still to be made in various earlier chapters. So it looks now as if I wouldn't get the whole thing in shape to be Xeroxed and sent to you on the date I'd hoped. But I still firmly intend to get it to you well in advance of our arrival.

This was the summer of the Watergate hearings, which Lindley mentions but Matthews seems oblivious of. He reports on May 30 the complications of delivering a manuscript across the Atlantic:

> Here it is. I had my much-patched copy xeroxed today at the Cambridge University Library, and the only paper they supply weighs a ton. I've cut down the weight a little by trimming the pages. It's not perfectly clean copy, but I hope not too messy to be acceptable. The only copy I have now is the one from which this one was xeroxed, so when you have this copied in New York, will you have one made for me? I can pick it up when I come over in July? The total needed is, I'm afraid, is considerably more than the three I mentioned when you were here. . . . I'll expect to be billed for all this xeroxing, of course.
> I'm told I should be feeling euphorious, or at least relieved. In fact I feel like a bank—robber on the run, expecting any day to see the Wanted signs pasted up in the post offices.

Lindley responded with enthusiasm:

> Oh dearest Tom, what glad tidings in the letter and telegram that arrived today. Can't wait! My notion then would be to xerox rapidly, shoot Cyrilly 2 copies, and discuss with her the matter of first serial here and in England. I think it ought, also to be considered by our legal dept, who are prepared to fight the claims of fair use all the way up to the Supreme Court. They may feel that release prior to book publication here could somehow weaken their case. Don't know; haven't a clue; will have to consult.

On June 21, she reports that "Our law man (a very dear, intelligent person) has read *Great Tom* and is, indeed, very relaxed about *fair use*." The lawyer asked for some reduction in the quoted material, but also, Lindley writes:

> Mostly what he wants are specific citations for all quoted passages, from everyone and everywhere, which is why I'm dashing this note off now. I'll send you his specific itemization as soon as it has been typed, but I thought I should alert you to the tedious prospect of rounding up all those effing references and, perhaps, start someone typing them. My notion would be NOT to produce footnotes, but to list AT THE BACK OF THE BOOK, THE SOURCES, Chapter by Chapter. I'm sending you a backbreaking example of how it's been done in another book.

Matthews responded that to do that he would have to bring "to the US all my files and about two shelves of books," and essentially refuses to undertake such an effort, "Whether I've missed the bus or not, can I face the prospect of giving up one of my last holidays with friends and family for a high-pressure rescue job in a place where all my nightmares still come from?"

Obviously, a compromise was reached, and the book was successfully published in spite of all the obstacles Matthews faced. His early detective work proved to be of great value to other biographers, even if some were frustrated by the absence of footnotes (the book does include references to published texts and a bibliography). Others disliked Matthews's easy, journalistic style. But no one could deny that *Great Tom* offered a unique view, drawn from a wide range of sources. Matthews himself was realistic about the limitations of his sources:

> Eyewitnesses, as we know, cannot always be wholly trusted: they contradict one another, they misremember or fail to see; sometimes they lie. Documents are simply eyewitnesses at one or more remove. A sleazy newspaper report, perhaps with some of its facts wrong or with their emphasis askew, ripens in time into "an invaluable firsthand account." In the case of such an elusive character as T. S. Eliot a biographer should be happy if, in the course of his struggles against failure, he can now and again strike bedrock, if only a glancing blow.[62]

Matthews's great contribution was to record the memories of people who had known Eliot, and to sift through the conflicting stories about his life and character. Matthews also managed to bring to light some information about women whose stories were at that point almost unknown.

Eliot's behavior towards people close to him has been a subject of interest for decades, not only in articles and books but in *Tom and Viv,* a play and then movie, in part instigated

---

62 *Great Tom,* p. xviii.

by the revelations about Vivien Eliot in *Great Tom*. Matthews's questions about John Hayward (Hayward himself had died in 1965) may have made matters more confusing; the debate over when and how TSE had told Hayward that he was going to marry his secretary continued long after *Great Tom*'s publication. Years later, Valerie Eliot was still defending her husband on this point.

The same question has arisen in connection with Emily Hale. In this case, we still face the kind of confusion Matthews tried, with limited success, to sort out in the Hayward-Eliot story. Did TSE inform Hale that he had changed his mind about the possibility of marriage and had engaged himself to someone else? Or did he let her find out from a newspaper article before hearing from him directly? The record is unclear.

The "memorandum" that forbade his widow to assist any biographer, which was attached to Eliot's will, is mentioned frequently in Matthews's letters and journal. It has never been published, and no authorized biography of T. S. Eliot has appeared. But we now know that the memorandum was dated September 30, 1963,[63] the same date as that on the final version of the so-called "Harvard" letter[64] in which Eliot discounted his relationship with Emily Hale and effusively praised Valerie Eliot. (This letter was published, by Eliot's written instructions, on January 2, 2020, hours after Princeton opened the Eliot-Hale archive to readers.) The connection between these two documents is something that would have intrigued T. S. Matthews and will no doubt interest future biographers.

---

63 Du Sautoy, Peter. "Eliot's Request." Letter to the *New York Review of Books*. April 15, 1976.
64 Morris, Leslie A. "T. S. Eliot on his letters to Emily Hale." Houghton Library, Harvard. January 2, 2020.

ABOUT THE AUTHOR

T. S. (Thomas Stanley) Matthews (1901–1991) was an American writer and editor who divided his time between the United States and England for many years. His early career as a journalist culminated with a period as editor of *TIME* magazine. After leaving *TIME* in 1953, he published a number of books, and was recruited to write the first major biography of T. S. Eliot, *Great Tom: Notes Towards the Definition of T. S. Eliot*, published by Harper & Row in 1973. He was a wealthy and well-connected man with friends on both sides of the Atlantic. He was able to make use of those connections when he undertook the difficult task of writing about Eliot. In an unusual reversal, he was also known later in life as one of the ex-husbands of American writer Martha Gellhorn, who was herself annoyed to be referred to as the ex-wife of Ernest Hemingway.

FOREWORD AUTHOR

Sara Fitzgerald's biography of Emily Hale will be published by Rowman & Littlefield in 2024. She is the author of *The Poet's Girl: A Novel of Emily Hale and T. S. Eliot.* Her essays about Hale's life have appeared in Volumes 3,4 and 5 of *The T. S. Eliot Studies Annual,* the 2020, 2022 and 2023 editions of the *Journal of the T. S. Eliot Society* (UK), and *Time Present* and *Exchanges,* the newsletters of the International T. S. Eliot Society and the British society, respectively. She has also presented papers on Hale and Eliot at conferences of the International T. S. Eliot Society, the South Atlantic Modern Language Association and the Midwest Modern Language Association. She is also the author of *Conquering Heroines: How Women Fought Sex Bias at Michigan and Paved the Way for Title IX* and *Elly Peterson: "Mother" of the Moderates,* both published by University of Michigan Press. She retired after a career in journalism that included fifteen years as an editor and new media developer for the *Washington Post.*

INDEX

A

Abels, Cyrilly 37, 53, 188–189, 213, 217
Acton, Harold 57
Adamson, Donald 146, 199
Aiken, Conrad 93, 110, 131
Aldous, William 72
All Souls' College 126, 129–130
Askwith, William 169
Ayer, Freddie 53

B

Baker, Bobby 192
Balfour, Michael 146
Barnes, Djuna 112–113
Barron, Stanley 208
Beerbohm, Henry Maximillian 51
Beinecke Library 113
Bell, John 65, 67, 69, 84, 87
Berlin, Isaiah 53, 121, 148
Betjeman, John 165
Binney, Elaine 29, 120
Blackwell, Kenneth 95, 127, 128
Blakiston, Noel 78–79, 124, 134
Bodleian Library 9, 48, 53, 126–227
Bond, W. H. 86, 94
Bowers, Fredson 202–203
Bowra, Maurice 53
Bradby, Christopher 149
Bridges, Robert 119
Broch, Hermann 190
Brown University 11, 36, 88
Budberg, Moura 116

C

Cambridge University Library 219
Cantwell, Bob 188
Carter, John 54, 195
Cecil, David 53, 189
Cheetham, Eric 180–181
Childs, Marquis 74
Clarendon Press 11, 58, 63, 82, 204
Clarke, Sir Ashley 187
Coghill, Nevill 33, 48, 170
Colefax, Lady 15–17
Colefax, Sybil 15
Connolly, Cyril 145
Cooper, Diana 16
Crossman, Richard 53, 82

D

Dane, Paul 165
Davin, D. M. 61
Davis, Greta 192
Deakin, F. W. 53, 57, 60, 82, 149
Dennis, Rodney 28
Diamond, Clifford 165
Dix, William S. 103
Dobrée, Bonamy 35
Doon, Rupert 194
Du Sautoy, Peter 81, 84, 87, 89, 91, 105, 179, 180
Dyke, Nathan 171, 175

E

Edel, Leon 22, 217
Eliot, Alexander 22

Eliot, Valerie Fletcher 10, 12, 22, 36, 49, 50, 55, 57, 75, 83–84, 120, 123, 131, 140–141, 166–168, 174, 179–181, 191, 214, 221–222
Eliot, Vivien(ne) Haigh-Wood 9, 11, 26–27, 35, 48, 89, 95, 173, 188, 196, 205, 209–211, 221
Elliott, Thomas 152
Ellmann, Richard 5, 148, 192
Elsmith, Dorothy 217
Eno, Alice 76
Evans, Walker 112–114

F

Faber & Faber 21–22, 47, 51, 65–67, 70–71, 75, 81, 84, 86, 89, 99–101, 104–105, 133, 144, 146, 152, 165, 167, 172, 191, 218
Faber, Geoffrey 164
Fabre, M. Michel 61–62
Cheetham, Father Eric 193–194
Fawcett, James 52, 62–65, 67, 69, 71, 82, 84, 87
Ferrar, John 32
Ferrar, Nicholas 32
Finley, John 98
Fitzgerald, Joan 186–187, 190
Footman, David 172
Fouljambes, Constance 194
Fowle, Anne 40, 106, 135, 147
Fowle, Chink 106
Frankel, William 51
Frost, Robert 3, 50

G

Gallup, Donald 27, 63, 93, 113, 166, 178–179

Gardner, Helen 58, 65–67, 114, 139, 141, 147–149, 203–204, 214
Garnett, David 50, 188
Garrett, Pat 48, 81, 143, 152, 171, 177, 183, 192, 202
Gellhorn, Martha 29, 223
Giroux, Bob 37, 217
Goldsmid, Sir Henry Avigdor 195
Grant, Duncan 188, 207
Guggenheim, Peggy 187, 190
Guinness, Alec 184

H

Haigh-Wood, Maurice 27, 106, 147, 150, 156, 165–166, 196, 198
Hale, Emily 4, 9, 10, 31, 49, 100, 103, 108, 110, 183–184, 192–193, 199–200, 202–203, 215, 217, 221–222, 225, 227
Hale, Nancy 193, 202–203
Hammond, Mason 187
Harding, D. W. 6
Harper & Row 26, 57, 74, 92, 97, 99, 118, 122–124, 126, 155, 188, 223
Hartley, L. P. 188
Hayter, Sir William 53
Hayward, John 11, 17, 29, 54–56, 120, 147, 154, 157, 169, 177, 180–181, 188, 195, 201, 206, 213, 221
Heaton, Wallace 209
Heimerd, Alan 98
Hemingway, Ernest 29, 223
Heston, Jeanne 183
Hinkley, Eleanor 38
Hirth, Mary 86, 97
Hofer, Philip 187
Holland, Frank 202

Holroyd, Michael 26
Hopkinson, Henry 76
Horne, John 192
Houghton Library 10, 28, 39, 70, 82, 86, 93, 98, 100, 108, 178, 187, 190, 205, 222, 227
Hutchinson, Mary 27
Hutchinson, St. John 27, 87, 88

I
Iselin, John Hay 96–97

J
Jabez-Smith, A. R. 168, 171–172, 175, 180
Joachim, Harold H. 152
John Hay Library 88

K
Kahler, Eric 190
Kauffer, E. McKnight 19
Kenner, Hugh 131
Kennerley, Morley 172
King, Cecil 195
King's College Library 10–11, 28, 30, 54, 70, 72, 82, 86, 116, 140, 151–153, 156, 164, 167, 201, 227
Kirk, Russell 165
Kronenberger, Louis 113

L
La Galliano, Eva 39
Lamb, Aimee and Rosamund Rosamund 29, 188-189
Lee, Laurie 54, 165
Lehman, Edward 23
Lehmann, John 23

Lehmann, Rosamond 22
Levine, Harry 112
Lewis, Cecil Day 54, 56
Lindley, Frances 36–37, 63, 70–71, 75, 100, 112, 121–122, 124–125, 131, 134, 154, 171, 189, 205, 213
Lipscomb, Thomas H. 123
London Library 82
Louise, Princess Marie 193
Lowell, Robert 112, 117–119

M
Mackenzie, Compton 89
Maclean, Alan 53, 68, 83, 85, 87, 104, 205, 208, 212
MacLeish, Archibald 93, 111, 153
Macmillan, Harold 84
Mairet, Philip 49, 70
Mansfield, Katherine 188
McCarthy, Desmond 152
McMaster University 94–95, 123, 127, 134
Millin, Sarah Gertrude 133
Milton Academy 153
Mitnik, Raymond 29
Monteith, Charles 65–66, 68, 84
Moore, Marianne 163, 186–187
Moore, Tommy 33
More, Paul Elmer 13, 15
Morley, Frank V. 47, 51, 66, 68
Morrell, Ottoline 159, 161, 168, 188
Morrell, Philip 87–88
Munby, A. N. L. 11, 86, 144, 151, 167, 180, 195, 201, 206, 211
Munnings, A. J. 152
Murray, John 33

N

Newby, Howard 218
New College 47, 155, 182
New York Public Library 28
Nicoll, John 204–205, 209
Nicolson, Harold 16

O

Oakeley, Diana 120, 170
Oliver, Colin 53, 70–72, 82, 86–87, 89, 91–92, 98, 174, 205
Oppenheimer, Herbert 88, 171, 175
Owen, Deborah 76, 104
Oxford Press 67, 69, 87, 100, 135, 139, 144, 216

P

Patmore, Brigit 199
Patmore, Derek 199
Perkins, John Carroll 100
Perlman, Moshe 164
Pindard, Mavis. E. 91
Pound, Ezra 12, 28, 56, 67, 137, 142, 186–187
Powell, H. W. H. Jr. 88
Pratt, Davis 190
Princeton University Library 103, 108, 215
Pritchett, V. S. 193

Q

Quinn, John 12, 28, 138, 140–142, 182

R

Randall, Sir Alec 156
Rees, Goronwy 194
Richards, I. A. 112, 137–138
Ridler, Ann 139, 149, 164
Ridler, Vivien 139
Robert, Isabel 187
Roberts, F. W. 96, 98
Roberts, Laurance 187
Roditi, Edouard 153
Rothermere, Esmond Cecil Harmsworth 195
Rothschild, Nathaniel Mayer Victor 30, 195
Rudge, Olga 186–187
Russell, Bertrand 56, 89, 95, 106, 109, 123, 127, 134, 157, 159–160, 163, 170
Russell, Vera 194–195
Ryders, Stephen 168

S

Sassoon, Siegfried 188
Scarth, G. H. 177
Sedgwick, Ellery 111–112
Sencourt, Robert 49, 57, 124, 146, 180–181, 191, 199
Shackleton, Robert 65, 67, 69, 210
Sherman, Stewart C. 88
Sinclair, Marjorie 21
Sitwell, Edith 200
Sitwell, Sacheverell 145, 197
Smith, Logan Pearsall 159
Sparrow, John 51, 62, 82, 126, 129–130, 155
Spencer, Ted 111
Spender, Stephen 57
Stafford, Jean 117
Storrs, Sir Ronald 16
Strachey, Lytton 26, 188
Sturtevant, Barbara 38, 107, 178
Sutro, John 57
Sweeney, Jack 112
Sykes, Christopher 69, 76, 117, 123–125, 134, 147, 218
Symonds, Arthur 54

T
Taylor, A. J. R. 53
Thayer, Lucy 198
Thayer, Scofield 197
Tilson, Nigel 137
Trevelyan, Hilda 125
Trevelyan, Mary 96, 125, 129, 147, 200, 203, 213, 215–217
Trilling, Lionel 216
Trinity College 192

U
University of California 153
University of Michigan Press 225
University of Minnesota 60, 102, 200–201
University of Texas 10–11, 28, 70, 82, 86, 96, 100, 205, 208
University of Virginia 193, 202

V
Valery, Paul 195
Vendler, Helen 138
Verdenal, Jean 61
Vinogradoff, Julien 208

W
Waldock, Humphrey 129
Washington University 27
Waugh, Evelyn 76
Weiner, Joyce 68, 72, 75, 89, 106
Weiner, Marjorie 174
Welch, Holmes H. 38, 178
Wertenbaker, Charles 193, 203
Wilson, Edmund 93, 108, 112, 164
Wilson, Elena 109
Wilson, Tim 150
Wolfson College 121, 148
Woolf, Leonard 27
Woolf, Virginia 27, 145, 208

ABOUT THE TYPE

Writing Great Tom was prepared from documents and letters written on typewriters. The main text is now set in a font called Special Elite, which mimics Smith Corona and Remington typewriter keys. The front and back matter are set in Century Schoolbook, which was designed by Morris Fuller Benton in 1924. The titles and headings are in Albertus, designed in the 1930s by Berthold Wolpe, who also designed many book jackets for Faber & Faber.

www.ingramcontent.com/pod-product-compliance
Lightning Source LLC
Chambersburg PA
CBHW061747290426
44108CB00028B/2918